HOW TO NET
A MILLION

Josephine Monroe

Prentice
Hall

An imprint of **Pearson Education**

London · New York · Reading, Massachusetts · San Francisco · Toronto · Don Mills, Ontario · Sydney · Tokyo
Singapore · Hong Kong · Seoul · Taipei · Cape Town · Madrid · Mexico City · Amsterdam · Munich · Paris · Milan

PEARSON EDUCATION LIMITED

Head Office:
Edinburgh Gate
Harlow CM20 2JE
Tel: +44 (0)1279 623623
Fax: +44 (0)1279 431059

London Office:
128 Long Acre
London WC2E 9AN
Tel: +44 (0)20 7447 2000
Fax: +44 (0)20 7240 5771

First published in Great Britain in 2000

© Pearson Education Limited 2000

ISBN 01-30-30751-3

Many of the designations used by manufacturers and
sellers to distinguish their products are claimed as
trademarks. Pearson Education Limited has made
every effort to supply trademark information about
manufacturers and their products mentioned in
this book.

British Library Cataloguing in Publication Data
A catalogue record for this book is available from the British Library.

10 9 8 7 6 5 4 3 2 1

Typeset by Land and Unwin (Data Sciences) Limited, Bugbrooke
Printed and bound in Great Britain by Biddles of Guildford and King's Lynn.

The publishers' policy is to use paper manufactured from sustainable forests.

CONTENTS

ACKNOWLEDGEMENTS

I WOULD LIKE TO THANK everyone who gave up some of their precious time for me to interview them – especially those I haven't had the decency to quote directly – and my mum, who lent me the money for the computer. I must also thank my fantastic partner, Geraldine Billam, who took care of business while I was writing.

INTRODUCTION

YOU'VE PROBABLY READ ABOUT SEVERAL Internet entrepreneurs in the past year who seem to have effortlessly turned a neat idea into a tidy profit. According to media myth, starting and running an Internet business goes something like this:

+ You have a great idea for a site;

+ You tell some friends who have lots of really relevant business experience and they think it's a great idea too;

+ You all have rich parents/savings/trust funds and are able to quit your jobs and get your fledgling website built before you get the business off the ground;

+ This overlaps with one of your management team having dinner with a venture capitalist who invests a few million quid for a 10 per cent equity stake in your company, giving your company a value of, say, £20 million;

+ The papers start writing about you; people visit your site in droves;

+ You float your company on the stock exchange for £200 million and you play tennis while an experienced MD is brought in to run the show;

+ At some point in the near future you are allowed to cash in your stock options and you never have to work again.

But, sadly, for most people it's a bit more like this:

- ✦ You have a great idea for a site;
- ✦ Your friends think you're mad and tell you you'd be crazy to follow your dream because what the hell do you know about the Internet anyway?
- ✦ You get hold of some free software from a CD you got with a net magazine and have a go at building your own site;

You need to resign yourself right now to the fact that it will be harder, take longer and you probably won't get as rich as you imagine.

- ✦ Your work your arse off;
- ✦ No one visits your site;
- ✦ You read countless articles in the business pages of newspapers about rich kids with useful parents raising millions in venture capital and curse everyone who ever went to Eton/Oxford/INSEAD;
- ✦ You know that *technically* the internet makes it possible for David to defeat Goliath, but you fear you're going to be squished by a giant at any second.

You need to resign yourself right now to the fact that it will be harder, take longer and you probably won't get as rich as you imagine. If it was as simple as building a website that people came to visit and queued up to advertise on, there wouldn't be a need for this book. But the truth is that setting up an e-business in the current gold rush climate requires sound technical knowledge, financial backing and marketing know-how. This will require most would-be entrepreneurs to learn at least three new languages – techie, money and bullshit. One minute you'll find yourself talking about JavaScript applications, the next chatting fluently about sensitivity analyses in key markets followed by a pitch to potential users/investors/advertisers about your best-thing-since-sliced-bread credentials. All the while you're worrying about how to register for VAT or wondering how to find a solicitor you can trust.

While this book can't give you useful parents, a degree from the right university or seed financing of a few hundred thousand pounds, it can help turn a bloody good idea into a nice little e-business. It can help you not dread a letter from the Inland Revenue and give you the basic knowledge to run a small business from book-keeping to registering as a limited company. And if you're good (and lucky) it might help make you rich.

While this book can't give you useful parents, a degree from the right university or seed financing of a few hundred thousand pounds, it can help turn a bloody good idea into a nice little e-business

It doesn't assume you have any knowledge of HTML or business practice and it doesn't contain any jargon or false promises. It's designed for the entrepreneur who has nothing but a good idea and the determination to see it through, and was born of my frustration in getting my own e-business, the-bullet.com, off the ground. But it's not based on my experience, but on interviews with countless other net entrepreneurs who have also staked everything – jobs, houses, relationships – on an e-dream and who have plenty of advice for those wishing to follow them. I have tried to speak to as many people as possible from the widest range of backgrounds: entrepreneurs, investors, marketing professionals, small business advisers, lawyers – basically anyone who could help new entrepreneurs make as few mistakes as possible. Their words are loaded with advice and caution and will be of help to anyone with dreams of internet success.

It's tougher than expected – everyone has said starting an e-business is the hardest thing they've ever done. Internet technology really does give the Davids of this world a chance to take on old industry giants. The message is clear that if you're smart, and lucky, it's still possible to make your fortune on the internet.

What's been most interesting is that whether I've been speaking to bedroom wannabes or MBA graduates with a few million in venture capital behind them, three clear themes have developed among the entrepreneurs:

✦ It's tougher than expected – *everyone* has said starting an e-business is the hardest thing they've ever done.

✦ There are no rules.

✦ Internet technology really does give the Davids of this world a chance to take on old industry giants.

The message is clear that if you're smart, and lucky, it's still possible to make your fortune on the internet.

Josephine Monroe
London, March 2000

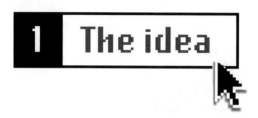

1 The idea

Coming up with an original idea for a website is a hard task. Already there are sites for cats who paint, or sites that have tips for pig farming, selling books and dealing in shares. Just about everything has already been covered. Some of them, clearly, have little chance of making money, and some of them are already producing million dollar turn-overs, but there is still a big chance to find a niche or a new application with which to make a fortune. While it's perfectly possible to build a website about anything – and this book will help you do that – if you want to make money you have to get real. What follows may seem a little tough – but if your expectations aren't realistic, you don't stand a chance.

Originality

'About 0.1 per cent of the business plans I get sent contain

an original idea,' says Tim Hammond, CEO of the incubator Ideas Hub. 'Everyone's always after that new application that changes the market, but the truth is that there are very, very few of them left.' Tim sees around 600 business plans a month and will invest in maybe 12 or so projects over the course of a year. You might think your idea is brand spanking new, but people like Tim who read thousands of plans see the same idea time and time again.

Even if you are absolutely sure that no one could possibly have had the same idea as you for a website, spend a few hours surfing through search engines and directories to try and find a rival, or even a near rival. There will almost certainly be one. If you're lucky it will be in another country or so amateur that you can be sure it poses little threat to the professional site you intend to put up against it . . . but if that's enough to convince you that there's a market for your idea, think again. You have to ask yourself why no one else is doing it. If it's such a good idea, why isn't someone else raking in those millions you're dreaming of right now? And even if you don't find a rival site, how can you be sure that someone with serious financial backing isn't developing a site right at this very moment? It's not enough to identify a new market; you have to be sure that your approach is unique and comprehensive.

Not all ideas have to be completely original to be successful, however. In the UK – or indeed anywhere outside the US – it's legitimate to look at thriving sites in America, nick the idea and try to capture the European market before the Yanks get here. This has advantages and disadvantages: investors and advertisers might be persuaded to get involved with your project because they see the merit in someone else's track record. But equally, smart folk know that no successful American company is going to let a rival take away its European market without a fight – and the chances are that they've got the brand and the money to take your project on and see it off.

The secret of successful so-called 'me too' ideas is to find the flaw in what your rivals are offering. A lot of emphasis is put on the so-called 'first mover advantage' but as Amory Hall of Web development agency methodfive.com says:

'The pioneers often get the arrows when the settlers get the land.' See how you can improve on what they offer. And then see how you can improve on it again. Being able to analyse a rival's offering really helps you develop your own, both in terms of content and attitude, which is vital, since being successful in a crowded market requires much more money. 'Firms are raising millions in venture capital and spending half of it on advertising just to get a toe in the market,' says Martin Fiennes of Top Technology, a UK investment firm. 'You have to be really sure that an idea can compete if it's the second or third to market otherwise you risk spending millions on advertising instead of the product … and the product will suffer.'

While it makes no sense to try and compete with Amazon or Bol selling books, that doesn't mean there isn't a market for online booksellers. 'If someone wants to specialise in biology textbooks, for example, and completely capture that specialist market then there might still be a case for investment,' says Fiennes.

Can your idea make money?

If you're looking just to make a living out of your site, then you might be happy to calculate a quick balance sheet with outgoings and earnings to decide if it's worth your while, but an investor will look at your idea with a completely different set of expectations. They might be willing to wait for up to 10 years to get a return on any investment, but they will only take the plunge if your idea can turn their £1 million investment into a £10 million or £100 million return. Five per cent interest is not what investors like – they like big numbers with lots of zeros on the end.

So let's just say you've got this great idea to sell biology textbooks online. You've set up a supply deal with a publisher which means you can undercut your high street rivals, you know you can deliver orders on time and you have such fantastic contacts with biology teachers that you know the orders will come. It might be a nice little business, but to turn it into a real money-spinner that will attract investment, you're going to have to think laterally, no matter what your idea is.

In this case, what else is there to offer? Ask yourself what people who buy biology textbooks may also want. Do they need help with revision or setting lessons, do they need the support of colleagues in other parts of the country? Are they interested in the latest biology news? If they are, how can you exploit these needs? You will have to offer all these services in addition to selling books to get their attention, and crucially to build some brand loyalty – you have to give them a reason to come back even if you don't have their desired book in stock. This is called protecting your market, covering all the bases to prevent rivals with better deals with textbook publishers coming at you. But to rake in the cash, you need to work out what else you can sell to them. What about magazine sub-scriptions, lab coats, travel to important conferences, anatomical posters to put up in classrooms . . . it doesn't matter how far away from your original idea you get, if it adds income to your site it's important. You also need to ask yourself who would want to advertise to reach your target market. An investor might ask you to name 10 potential advertisers off the top of your head. Can you? And of those advertisers, which can you act as an affiliate for (a deal where you take a percentage – typically less than 10 per cent – if someone buys their product through your site)? Will your service be free to users and just make money from advertising, or – as long as it's not an e-commerce proposition – will it be so compelling that you can charge a subscription fee?

Suddenly, it doesn't sound like your nice little business selling textbooks any more, and your good idea has turned into a global operation that requires everything from sourcing rare books in Brazil to organising bus trips to Birmingham. It's so big that you will probably need partners to fulfil different parts of the service. If this scares you, then internet entrepreneurism probably isn't for you. You certainly won't get rich. But if this excites you and you've brainstormed the hell out of your idea to identify every possible revenue source, then you are ready to really start finding out if it's an idea that's worth pursuing. But that's only if you can answer 'yes' to the next question: are you the best person to do it?

Are you up to the job?

You don't need this book to ask you if you've got the appetite to be an entrepreneur. Every glossy leaflet you pick up from high street banks when you open a business account will ask you if you're capable of working through minor illnesses and taking rejection. Obviously you need a tough skin to survive, but there are no real rules about who makes a good internet entrepreneur. Some of the richest people in the business are geeks who can hardly speak to strangers but can write fantastic software programs. Some are experts in PR but their products have little substance.

While bloody-mindedness will never go amiss in almost any line of business, the magic of technology means we don't all have to talk the talk to walk the walk, as it were. You can approach people via email, make contacts from carefully reading the trade press or by searching companies' websites for biographies of employees. It's much easier to get to the right people and approach them in the right way thanks to the web – bright braces and breezy attitudes don't always help to get you noticed.

If you do want to take a psychometric test to prove to yourself that you've got an appropriately entrepreneurial personality you can find a good one at *http://www.bsos. umd.edu/socy/rosenberg.htm*. But be prepared to say 'yes' to questions like 'I rarely have trouble concentrating on something for a long time' or 'no' to 'A sure way to be disappointed is to want something too much'.

The real questions you have to ask yourself are as follows:

1. Have I got the time to see this through?
2. If I have to give up work, can I make enough money at it in the short term to see me (and my family) through?
3. Have I really got the contacts to make it happen?

You must not underestimate how time-consuming starting a business – any business – is. Your partner will make demands on your time, as will your friends, or your children if you have them. If you start working from 7am to midnight seven days a week you will probably have to sacrifice the quality of some of your relationships. Ask yourself if you're prepared to do this and if the people around you will be supportive, or jealous of the fact that your new project takes you away from them.

And don't underestimate either how hard it is being poor. If there's going to be a period between giving up work and the money coming in – and be prepared for this stage to go on longer than you think – you might be living on a fraction of your current income. Is this feasible?

But the most important question of the three is the last. It will be your contacts and your ability to form alliances with suppliers, users and advertisers that will single out your idea, your business plan and ultimately your website for success. But you don't have to do it on your own . . .

Making friends

'One of the biggest mistakes I've seen entrepreneurs make is not wanting to work with other people. If they think they can do it all alone, or won't give up equity to get partners on board, I can be pretty sure they won't stay in business,' warns Tim Hammond.

It can be pretty galling to realise that to get people to work with you you're going to have to give them a stake in your company. After all, it's your idea. But it's unlikely that you've got all the skills and contacts needed to make your idea work – and if you don't work with people who have, you could end up owning 100 per cent of nothing. While you might think one per cent should be enough to entice people to join you – after all, it's a brilliant idea – they might be after 50 per cent. This obviously isn't nice, but keep in mind that Jeff Bezos, the founder of Amazon, only owns a minority stake of his company. And his share is still worth billions.

To make any internet venture fly – and possibly more crucially to convince investors you're worth the risk – you need to be able to offer the following things: expertise in your chosen field, financial management skills, technical know-how and some method of guaranteeing an income. If you have the sector expertise but have never run a company before, look around your circle of friends and colleagues to see if they have accountancy skills, design skills or are capable of selling advertising space. Forming a team with a complementary skill set can be invaluable for a number of reasons. For starters you might be able to raise enough money between you to get your idea to the next stage. But more crucially than money, fresh minds from different industries can really help you see the potential of your idea – and the pitfalls – from different angles.

For investors, one of the most crucial deciding factors when considering putting money into ventures is the strength of the management team, so you might want to keep in mind the following: are these people really the best you can get; can you work together; do you want the same things?

Amory Hall of methodfive says that:

'Although we always want to work on projects with strong management teams, it sometimes becomes apparent that teams of four of five can be quite unstable. Often they want different things for the company. Sometimes one person has put all the seed financing in and just wants a return, sometimes they can't decide who's in charge. It's important that everyone on the management team has exactly the same vision for the company otherwise they will fall out and jeopardise the whole project by pulling it in different directions.'

You should also assemble an advisory board. This can be reasonably informal at this stage but you need to approach key people who can offer you advice on a regular basis. On your advisory board you want professionals with different skills, contacts and expertise: ideally you want respected figures in their fields. If you're lucky you will have the personal contacts to approach MDs, strategists and sales specialists, but if you don't, ask around or do a bit of cold-calling. As well as giving you the benefit of their experience, your advisory board can act as ambassadors for you when you get going and introduce you to the right people.

But what happens if you can't find all the necessary skills – or the seed financing – among your friends and you're still absolutely convinced your idea is a winner? Well, there is help available through small business advisers and incubators who specialise in putting teams together, but you're still not ready to go to them unless you can tick all of the following boxes:

Is your idea different from anything else in the marketplace? ☐

Is it different enough to compete with what's already on offer? ☐

Have you brainstormed every possible revenue stream? ☐

Do you have the contacts to make it work? ☐

Have you got the time and resources to give it your best shot? ☐

Directory

The following websites have been selected to give you a good introduction into internet entrepreneurialism. They range from news sites to advice centres to dictionaries of web jargon. They will help put your idea into perspective.

http://e-comm.webopedia.com/
Glossary of internet jargon

http://www.strikingitrich.com
Read how other people made it

http://www.helensface.com
The face that launched a thousand ships – and maybe a

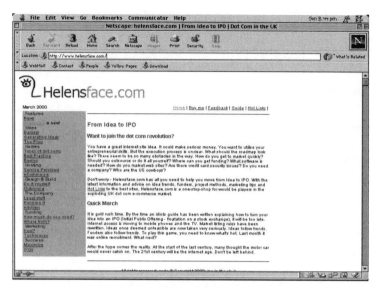

Inside the browser window:

File Edit View Go Bookmarks Communicator Help

Netscape: helensface.com | From Idea to IPO | Dot Com in the UK

Back Forward Reload Home Search Netscape Images Print Security Stop

Location: http://www.helensface.com/   What's Related

WebMail Contact People Yellow Pages Download

Helensface.com

March 2000   Home | Buy me | Feedback | Guide | Hot Links |

Features
News
_____ is new!
Ideas
Games
Generating Ideas
The Plan
Names
Types of dot coms
Best Practice
Buying
Hosting
Service Providers
eCommerce
- Design & Build
- Do it yourself
Outsourcing
The Company
Legal stuff
Funding it
Advisers
Funding
How much do you need?
Where from?
Marketing
How?
Techniques
Success
Maximize
IPOs

From Idea to IPO

Want to join the dot com revolution?

You have a great internet site idea. It could make serious money. You want to utilise your entrepreneurial skills. But the execution process is unclear. What should the roadmap look like? There seem to be so many obstacles in the way. How do you get to market quickly? Should you outsource or do it all yourself? Where can you get funding? What software is needed? How do you market web sites? Are there credit card security issues? Do you need a company? Who are the US cowboys?

Don't worry - Helensface.com has all you need to help you move from Idea to IPO. With the latest information and advice on idea trends, funders, project methods, marketing tips and Hot Links to the best sites, Helensface.com is a one-stop-shop for would be players in the exploding UK dot com e-commerce market.

Quick March

It is gold rush time. By the time an idiots guide has been written explaining how to turn your idea into an IPO (Initial Public Offering - floatation on a stock exchange), it will be too late. Internet access is moving to mobile phones and the TV. Market listing rules have been rewritten. Ideas once deemed unfeasible are now taken very seriously. Ideas follow trends. Funders also follow trends. To play this game, you need to know what's hot. Last month it was online recruitment. What next?

After the hype comes the reality. At the start of the last century, many thought the motor car would never catch on. The 21st century will be the internet age. Don't be left behind.

---

thousand businesses. This UK site has plenty of information and useful links for would-be millionaires

http://www.kickstartventures.com
Excellent resource of news, links and advice for entrepreneurs

http://www.firsttuesday.com
Subscribe to the mailing list of the best known networking event organiser

http://www.boobnight.co.uk
Much more informal networking group – so you could be talking to anyone. It stands for **B**uy **O**ur **O**wn **B**eer, in case you were wondering

http://theglasshouse.moonfruit.com
One of the more recent networking forums that meets monthly in London

http://www.iwks.com
The website for *Internet Works*, a monthly magazine for small and medium sized e-businesses

http://www.fourleaf.com
Established networking site where you can also get sound professional advice on legal and other business matters

http://edge.lowe.org/
Help for the budding entrepreneur

http://www.123workskills.freeserve.co.uk
A whole site dedicated to improving your time and resource management skills

http://www.new-business.co.uk
As the URL says, a site for people like you

http://www.knowthis.com
Major research resource with lots of links to useful sites with info on everything from promotion to legal matters

http://www.ecommerceadvisor.com/
Get your questions answered by the e-commerce advisor, also contains lots of articles and valuable advice

http://www.ibm.com/e-business/what/how/index.html
Tips on setting up an e-business

http://netb2b.com/educational_tracks/
Articles from Net Marketing on setting up a website

http://www.internet.com
Twelve channels of everything internet on this major US network. **http://uk.internet.com/** is the UK version

http://www.trainingpages.co.uk
A searchable database of courses available in the UK for business and IT training needs, from Photoshop and Dreamweaver to marketing and financial management

http://www.worldwidelearn.com
A kind of online correspondence course in every subject you may need for your business. A fee is payable and the company is US based

1. Name(s)

Ollie Cornes (Co-founder & CEO)
Alf Nwawudu (Co-founder & CEO)
Damien Webster (Co-founder)

2. Age(s)

27
27
26

3. URL of your business

www.hobomedia.com
www.hobomusic.com

4. What is the purpose/nature of your business/website?

HoboMedia is creating a business to business community for the professionals in the music industry. Our company's goal is to 'Make Music-Making Easier.' This will be achieved using the hobomusic.com website which was launched in May.

5. Date your business started

The original ideas were germinated in November 1998, the company was formed in March 1999. We received venture funding in March 2000.

6. Is this your first new media venture?

Yes.

7. Briefly describe your previous business experience and state how useful this was in starting your site

OLLIE: I am a technology nut – I love technology – the speed it moves at and the way it solves problems. My career has been with technology within a number of small internet-related companies over the last six years as a programmer and systems manager/analyst. In 1997 I began to satisfy a desire to know why some people are successful and some are not. The knowledge I gained through the books I read and the people I met since then has been a great help to me as that knowledge is now being put into practice. I think skills are almost irrelevant in a start-up – the important factor is your attitude and your ability to develop the skills needed.

ALF: I've always been into business, and I think going into emerging market analysis and trading helped because you get to believe that companies can grow. On a business trip to Asia I saw that what was once wasteland had become, in 20 years, huge wealth-producing areas. In some ways this helped me believe that I could make a difference in my lifetime. Being an analyst helped more directly because I got to know the language of business and understand what makes companies succeed or fail in the financial world. It has been useful but when your own hands are on the steering wheel things look very different.

DAMIEN: On leaving college I found myself working straight away in a start-up environment as one of the core team members in a company that went on to become a leading new media company. I have seen first-hand how the internet has become an incredibly powerful and sophisticated business tool for an increasingly more demanding and wider audience. Those three proved invaluable, they enabled me to get a very good insight into some of the hidden pitfalls that start-up companies inevitably fall into no matter how well prepared they may be. I also learnt how you deal with these situations in a positive manner and actually learn from them. Due to the ever evolving nature of the Internet you find yourself constantly having to adopt new skills; more importantly, you have to have an open mind and the willingness to do so.

8. Briefly outline your educational qualifications. Please state which universities/colleges you got these qualifications from.

OLLIE: Four A-levels and I went to Durham University where I studied Computer Science. I am also a Microsoft Certified Systems Engineer. However my most important skills for HoboMedia are calmness, persistence, intelligence, motivation and energy.

ALFIE: Four A-levels – Woolwich College (Maths, Physics, Economics, Computer Science). BA Economics – St Johns College, Cambridge.

DAMIEN: Three A-levels, then I went to Newham College to study graphic design, however the majority of my time was spent working on multimedia based projects which on leaving enabled me to get into the emerging new media environment/workplace.

9. Were you able to/did you try to raise seed financing from family and friends? If so, how much did you raise?

Between the three of us, including the salaries we were not paid, we invested approximately £250,000. The actual cash injected came from credit cards, overdrafts, short-term contract work and family/friends. We put about £30,000 cash into the business.

10. Did you have any useful contacts when it came to raising finance? If so, what kind of introductions proved to be the most useful?

The company that provided our first major round of financing (Brainspark) was introduced to us by Adam Twiss at Zeus (*zeus.com*). Ollie met Adam through Damien Reeves, the other Zeus guy, who is a friend from a previous job where Damien worked as a programmer.

11. Roughly how much money did you raise in venture capital and was this enough?

Brainspark invested approximately half a million pounds in HoboMedia in exchange for a minority equity stake. The money given is never enough!! It'll get us to where we need to be in six months and focuses our minds.

12. How many people were there on your management team?

HoboMedia has four directors – Ollie, Alf and Damien, plus Stewart Dodd, the CEO of Brainspark. HoboMedia also has an advisory panel comprising a number of music industry and business achievers – the 'grey hairs.'

13. How useful have you found networking events like First Tuesday and BoobNight?

These events did not help us a great deal.

14. What would you do differently if you had to start all over again?

Take more advice from people who had done it before. Create structures earlier, be more careful, make more plans. But to be honest, we've had a fabulous time and have learnt a massive amount. We've made a lot of costly mistakes, but each has been our teacher. We don't regret anything in particular – every cloud has a silver lining, and every turd was once a nice lunch!

15. What do you think are the criteria that have most helped you make a success of your business (e.g. having first mover advantage, a brilliant marketing campaign, bloody-mindedness)?

The principles of our company are R.I.S.E. – Relationships, Integrity, Simplicity, Excellence. Those are very important, as are a sense of fun, extreme persistence, and looking on the bright side when the chips are down. The relationship between the three founders/directors is vital; that is something we work hard at.

16. What's been the hardest thing you've had to face since starting your business?

The possibility in late 1999 that the whole project might have to be abandoned after a year of very hard work.

17. What's the most useful piece of advice you've been given?

There are so many!
◆ Most Business People are SHITS – Show High Interest Then Stall (don't let procrastination deter you).

- Don't do things on favours, get contracts in place as soon as possible.
- Learn from your mistakes.
- Stay motivated but leave your ego behind.
- Stay calm, be patient.
- READ like a book addict.
- Work as hard on developing yourself as you do on the job.
- Never forget about the people that you're selling to.
- Have a CEO.

18. What's the one piece of advice you wish someone had given you, but didn't?

'Everything will take four times longer than you expect,' but we wouldn't have believed them so there would have been no point them saying it. The suggestion in the question is that there is a short-cut to becoming successful – this is not true. Success is the reward for hard work and determined, focused effort. There is no way to overtake that process.

19. Do you believe it's still possible for someone with only a good idea and determination to succeed in new media – or is it all about raising money these days?

Determined people always succeed, quite simply because they never give up. In that respect, nothing has changed.

20. Are you in profit?

No.

2 Market research

FINDING OUT AS MUCH AS you can about the market you want to enter will be vital to your success. You need to gather information about your potential users and find out the best way to reach them. Thorough market research is essential for three very powerful reasons:

1. It will help you develop a better business.

2. It will help you convince an investor about your business (and you can be sure that any venture capitalist will thoroughly research the market before handing over the cash – and it would be embarrassingly fatal for them to discover huge holes in your research).

3. It will prevent you from making hundreds of mistakes.

The information you gather now will form an essential part of your business plan, but it will also help you adapt your idea to achieve the maximum amount of profit. As you seek out your potential users and potential rivals, you will come across many ways to improve your offering and refine your pitch. If you overlook this vital step you risk wasting your time on a project that stands little chance of survival.

You will need to create a plan of action. Set yourself a range of objectives and make sure you answer all your own queries. You need to find out what rivals are out there, how your service will differ from theirs, how big the potential market is and what percentage of that market is online. Unfortunately there's no one place you can go to for this information and it can be a hard slog with few rewards. But think of it like decorating: this is the preparation work that makes that final coat of emulsion go on like a dream and looks like you got professional decorators in.

Search engines

You are going to be spending a lot of time online as you prepare to launch your site so now's the time to make use of one of those promotional offers that give you your first 100 hours online for free or switch to an unmetered provider. The most obvious place to start your market research is with the search engines.

Imagine you're looking for your – as yet unbuilt – site. What would you type into a search engine to find the services you intend to offer? Look to using as many different search engines as possible, including local search engines and meta ones. Don't just look at the first 10 sites you're offered, look at the first 100. Just because a site is number 75 on the list it doesn't mean it's useless. (Poor rankings don't necessarily indicate a poor site – if you'd put in different search criteria it might have come out on top.)

Have a look at every site that caters for your target market. See if they are a rival or a potential partner. Try and work out who their suppliers are and take a careful look at who advertises. If you think they offer a good service, work out how you can improve on it. Finding rivals is usually a good thing as it can help you focus better on your offering. Maybe you'll realise that you need to concentrate on one part of the market, or create a brand that identifies you as cool rather than comprehensive. Having a very strong idea of what will make your site different or better is going to help you when you come to build your site and eventually when you promote it.

Analyse what you like and don't like about potential rival sites. See how easy they are to navigate and look carefully for services you need to include in your offering. Then go back a week later and see if the site has been updated or maintained. If you spot a rival that has a counter of the number of visitors on it, go back in a week and see what the counter has increased by. Knowing the traffic your rivals is getting may help you assess the kind of traffic levels you're likely to get. If they have a mailing list, join it.

You have to know everything there is to know about your rivals. Try and find out how much they charge for advertising, if they've done any market research on their users and what their plans are for the future. Pretend to be a potential advertiser and get them to send you their media pack.

Trade press

Now is the time to start reading the trade press religiously. Almost every activity has its own publication, as does every industry. So whether your site is about macramé or the oil business, subscribe to the relevant magazine or newspaper now. Scan them for possible contacts or news of possible rivals. Look at the adverts too – these are the companies you will want to approach for advertising as soon as your site is up and running.

The other thing trade publications can help you find out is the size of your potential market. Why not phone up their advertising department and again pretend to be a potential advertiser: find out what their circulation is, what the demographic profile of their readership is and how much they charge. Obviously be discreet, but this information will be vital as you calculate the size of the market and the kind of rates you're going to have to set for advertising to lure sponsors to your site. You should also check out the Audit Bureau of Circulations site (*www.abc.org.uk*) which lists the circulation information of nearly 4,000 UK magazines. All the information you can lay your hands on will help you convince others about the viability of your business, as well as your serious intentions about running that business properly.

As well as keeping on top of what's happening in your chosen field, you'll need to start reading up on the internet business too. Magazines like *NewMediaAge* are essential to entrepreneurs. They are full of news about site launches, difficulties other entrepreneurs have had to face and opinions about the latest coding tricks or designs.

Reading internet magazines and industry sites is doubly important if you've never worked in new media before. It will help you identify the major players and give you an understanding of the way new media operates. The first few issues you read will probably make as much sense as logarithm tables, but you will start to see patterns and absorb valuable information. Treat it like homework so that when you finally start talking to people about your site you sound competent and clued-up.

 ## The internet

As well as looking for rival sites, you should also look at the sites listed in the directory for this chapter as there are countless organisations constantly conducting research that will be valuable to you. Whether it's making pre-dictions about the growth of e-commerce or analysing your particular market, somewhere out there is a site that's loaded with information to make your business plan irresistible to investors.

Personal contacts

While you don't want to give your plans away to people in the sector you want to exploit – they might tell their contacts – you need to sound out some key people about what they think of your plan. Be discreet: pretend to think the opposite of what you do ('I've heard that so-and-so is planning to throw their job in to launch a website' etc.) to gauge people's reactions. This is often the best way of finding out what's really going on.

You have to be very honest with yourself at this point: if you don't have the personal contacts to do market research effectively, do you honestly think you've got the contacts to make a successful site?

Using your head

Think laterally about places you can go to for further information. Is there a trade union or membership club associated with your target market? If there is, get in touch and find out how many members they've got. If your site will target a particular industry, phone up key companies and find out if their staff have access to the Internet or email. Gather as much information as you can about the size of your market and ascertain whether the people you need to reach are online.

If your site is creating a new market or changes the way businesses operate then this research will be harder. You may have to consider commissioning a research firm to come up with figures for you if your contacts can't give you a good approximation of the size of the market for your site.

Suppliers

There is another key element you need to research before you launch into building a site or seeking venture capital, and that's the supply chain that will keep your site full of the best products, journalism or prices.

If you intend to sell goods you don't manufacture yourself, you will need to set up deals with wholesalers and manufacturers. You may need to tie them into exclusive deals, or at least get some kind of confirmation from them that they will – if you get the funding – supply you with certain goods at certain prices. If you then need to deliver goods, you will need to form another partnership with a delivery company.

If the content of your site is going to be constantly updated then you need to find someone to write this if you can't do it yourself. Part of your research will involve identifying people you would like to employ as well as finding out the going rates for their services.

To find out if you're ready to move on to the next step, you must be able to answer 'yes' to the following questions:

Have you identified every possible rival? ☐

If there is no rival, are you convinced that this isn't because there is no future in your idea? ☐

Are you completely convinced that your idea is sufficiently different or better than any competitor? ☐

Do you know how big your target market is? ☐

Do you know what percentage of that market is online? ☐

Have you identified potential advertisers? ☐

Do you have enough feelers out to know if someone is planning to launch a rival site before you get yours off the ground? ☐

Do you have good enough contacts to ensure the necessary supply chain for your site? ☐

Directory

These market research sites have been selected because they contain either information or advice that can help you identify your market, and then attack it.

http://www.mckinseyquarterly.com
Free subscription to McKinsey articles on research into every industry

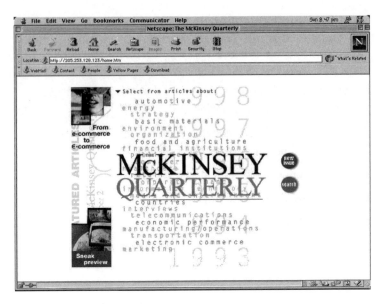

http://www.nua.ie/surveys/

Research on everything internet-related, including audience share and online ad spend trends

http://www.emarketer.com/

Facts and figures to help make an assessment of your chosen customer/audience potential

http://ecommerce.internet.com/

Features about the latest trends from Internet.com

http://cyberatlas.internet.com

Another service from internet.com, giving you a complete

breakdown of global web statistics and the latest market research

http://www.internet-sales.com/hot/
Full demographics and a guide to advertising trends on the internet – more UKcentric

http://www.mediametrix.com
Lots of statistics including a chart of the most visited websites

http://e-comm.webopedia.com/
Find out what all the e-commerce jargon means

http://www.planetit.com/techcenters/e-commerce/
News and trends, comment and analysis

http://www.ons.gov.uk/
The official figures for UK business from the Office of National Statistics

http://www.keynote.co.uk/
Provides a combination of market analysis, commentary, statistics and forecasts. You can look at the executive summary of each report for free

1. Name

Mike Barratt

2. Age

42

3. URL of your business

WeddingGuideUK.com

4. What is the purpose/nature of your business/website?

We provide a definitive and comprehensive source of information and advice about weddings online, offering products and services relevant to the occasion.

5. Date your business started

October 1996.

6. Is this your first new media venture?

No, I set up Associated Computing Ltd. back in 1985 to provide software programming services.

7. Briefly describe your previous business experience and state how useful this was in starting your site.

I was involved in a business that provided products and services to customers and suppliers alike, ensuring a high quality of customer care and saw the net as an excellent source of information fast!

I was interested in the speed at which both individuals and businesses were looking towards the net as a source of information and means to purchase products. I concluded that the internet offered tremendous growth potential and decided to start creating an internet service.

My wife was involved in weddings and this provided a source of information to start a website – it was obvious at the time that there was the potential to exploit the wedding market in that there were brides-to-be out there who needed support, guidance and information in a way that only the net could provide.

8. Briefly outline your educational qualifications. Please state which universities/colleges you got these qualifications from.

Honours degree in Environmental Services at University of East Anglia, Norwich 1982.

9. Were you able to/did you try to raise seed financing from family and friends? If so, how much did you raise?

I initially used personal savings to start the business, working evenings and weekends to develop content and create the forums for visitors to share thoughts and seek information. This was done to ensure that there was no dilution of equity and allow for 100 per cent ownership when looking for investment opportunities.

10. Did you have any useful contacts when it came to raising finance? If so, what kind of introductions proved to be the most useful?

No, I did not have any contacts. I was initially contacted by Freeserve who were interested to acquire the business; however, I ultimately selected venture capital from a small consortium of investors due to the ongoing support they were able to provide.

11. Roughly how much money did you raise in venture capital and was this enough?

£4 million; yes.

12. How many people were there on your management team?

None. I had support from external people plus a small committed team of copywriters, graphic designers and operational personnel.

13. How useful have you found networking events like First Tuesday and BoobNight?

I have never used them though I was aware of their presence.

14. What would you do differently if you had to start all over again?

Be more prepared for the VC process and the implications of time i.e. I would want to see more urgency in the approach which I believe would be more beneficial to the business and site – speed is essential in the growth of an Internet business, particularly in the light of any competition that may appear on the market.

15. What do you think are the criteria that have most helped you make a success of your business (e.g. having first mover advantage, a brilliant marketing campaign, bloody-mindedness)?

A belief that content and service excellence underwrite success and that the customer is always right.

16. What's been the hardest thing you've had to face since starting your business?

Taking the jump from being a one-man band driving the business on my own initiative to being involved in the expansion of a fast-growing business with all the cultural changes that occur; thinking as a big company with more people, extra responsibilities, time management issues and the need to accommodate all those changes.

17. What's the most useful piece of advice you've been given?

Do not lose faith, stay focused and you will succeed.

18. What's the one piece of advice you wish someone had given you, but didn't?

I would have appreciated more advice on expansion issues with venture capitalists, the processes involved and the implications of expansion on my business, and to be more aware of the length of time from the initial approach to the implementation. Do not underestimate the personal sacrifice and commitment needed to make this happen.

19. Do you believe it's still possible for someone with only a good idea and determination to succeed in new media – or is it all about raising money these days?

There is still a lot of opportunity for success in new media, but it is becoming increasingly important to back a 'good idea' with a sound business plan that shows a full understanding of your product or service, the competition and all the issues involved in setting up a business in a volatile market to secure that all-important investment capital. UK venture capital is not rich with internet talent and until very recently investors were less than supportive. US investment and capitalisation of new media businesses has stimulated a belated interest. It is still very difficult to get seed capital from investors without losing control of the business and inevitably their involvement changes the natural evolution of the business due to their commercial aspirations.

20. Are you in profit?

The external investment took place in January. We are rapidly expanding our operations and as such are not in profit.

3 Building your website

ONCE YOU'VE THOROUGHLY RESEARCHED YOUR idea you will be in a position to either start building your site or start raising finance, depending on the scope and scale of your site. Sadly though, even the best ideas have difficulty in getting the attention of investors unless they are being developed by people with a track record. Often the only way to get venture capital is to build a business without it. If you can prove your idea works then investors will be much more interested in your plan because you are eliminating much of the risk. This might mean having to build your website yourself.

Unfortunately, building a website yourself isn't easy – although it's far from impossible. Ideally you will have someone on your management team with the skills to be able to do this and, if you don't, you should really start looking for someone now. Of course, there are web design companies advertising in every net magazine and it's perfectly possible to outsource your web design, but the internet boom has meant countless web design companies have sprung up in the past year, often founded by people with little design or business experience. And the demand for designers means that prices are going up all the time. If you've got the money you can take your chances and choose a company, but be careful: there are some sharks out there. Unfortunately it is impossible for a book like this to recommend individual firms, but below there is plenty of advice about employing the right design agency. Even if you have no intention of building your site yourself, to instruct a designer efficiently you are going to have to learn a bit about site building yourself.

The best way to do this – and to find out how you want your site to look – is by surfing and looking at other people's sites, whether the content's got anything to do with your business or not. Don't just look at the design, look at the functionality: how easy is it to get from one page to another, how easy is it to find what you want? Have a good look at some of the page furniture, from the date to graphics and logos to menu bars. Are there little gimmicks like votes and searches that you want to have on your site? Are there things that you hate, like frames – when you get scroll bars in the middle of the screen – or pages that have too much text or too many images? Although you might think that a site looks fantastic because you find moving graphics exciting, imagine that you're visiting the site for the third time and decide whether you want an efficient site rather than a clever one. Start making a wish list and form an idea in your head of how someone will use your site. It will help to start drawing a storyboard on paper of how you think your site will look and behave. Sketching on paper also helps you realise how much data you can get on one screen and forces you to think logically about how your site will work.

There is nothing too technical in this chapter, and it's been written to be understood by someone with no design or technical knowledge. Even if you have no intention of building your site yourself and skipping to the Instructing a Web Designer section, reading the next section will help you get the most out of a designer – and should ensure that when you do talk to designers you know when they're talking crap!

Building it yourself

Planning

Spend several hours just thinking about what you want your site to do. Your business might be selling sausages, but you don't just want customers to come and buy sausages. You want them to trust your brand, value your service and recommend your sausages to their friends. If you want people to spend online you will have to work hard to make your customers trust you with their credit card details, so think carefully about creating the right image.

Imagine you are a customer and work out everything you would want to be told about your product and your service – whether that's the ingredients of your black puddings or an email confirming an order within seconds of placing it. Answer the following questions as fully as possible and keep them handy as they will inform you as you set about building your site:

1. What do I want my website to achieve (e.g. increased sales, greater brand awareness, better customer service etc.)?

2. Who am I trying to reach with my website? (Make sure you have a clear profile of your users and a method of reaching them.)

3. When do I want to launch my website? (Be realistic, but deadlines are the best motivator.)

4. How much money is it worth me spending on developing a website?

The basics

Most web pages are built using HTML (HyperText Markup Language) code. This doesn't require special software and can be written in Notepad (in Windows) or Simple Text (on Macs) and is read by a standard browser like Netscape Navigator or Internet Explorer (IE). HTML is essentially a series of tags that tells your browser what to do, be it getting an image from a certain source or linking to another page. HTML is really the cement that bonds images, text and navigational features together.

You can find several online tutorials (listed in the directory at the end of this chapter) that will take you through the basics of coding HTML. There are even sites where you can use ready-made templates to build your site, although these aren't a serious option for people wanting to create a professional impression. There are also books you can buy and courses you can go on. If you intend to build your site yourself it is ABSOLUTELY VITAL that you, or someone on your team, understands HTML – even if you intend to use an editing program like Go Live or Dreamweaver as these packages are all still imperfect and code knowledge is required to smooth all the edges.

In reality though, most DIYers use an HTML authoring package without raw code knowledge. Packages like FrontPage and PageMill are often part of software bundles handed out with new computers these days (FrontPage Express is included with Internet Explorer 5), but if you've never done any web design before it's probably worth investing in a good WYSIWYG (What You See Is What You Get) authoring program that lets you build pages exactly as they appear in a browser. Buying new software will usually give you access to a phone helpline for three months after purchase, and of course, new software comes with a manual, which is useful. Read reviews of authoring and editing programs in the net press and look out for freebies on the CDs that come with those magazines.

Keep in mind that those freebies don't come with a handbook and that you're not going to get a program that normally retails for £300 for free. You might just get a 30-day trial or a save-disabled version – but it's a good way of finding out your aptitude for web design without shelling out lots of money.

If you're using a Mac, be prepared for most of these freebies to be for PC users only. Also be prepared for anything you design on a Mac to look different when a PC user looks at it. PCs generally make text much bigger and you don't have absolute control over exactly how your site will look. Equally, if you're designing on a PC keep in mind that small print will be illegible on a Mac. (This problem is exacerbated by the peculiar habits of Netscape and IE which read code slightly differently.)

All any authoring software program will do is create the HTML code for you. You will still need to produce graphics in another application like Photoshop, Fireworks or Illustrator. Getting the software you want could set you back over £1,000 – something worth considering when you might find a designer to do it for you for less.

Obviously it's possible to get hold of pirated software and there are newsgroups which claim to offer tips on how to prevent time-limited trials ever expiring. There are also beta (not fully tested) versions of software available to download from some of the sites in this chapter's directory – so it is possible to get everything you need for free. You just have to weigh up if you can afford the time it will take you to get to grips with the software – especially if you eventually end up admitting defeat and calling in an expert.

To keep the various software packages open at one time, you will need a PC or Mac with at least 64Mb of RAM, but probably 128Mb. You will also want a fast processor (Pentium II or III on a PC or 400Mhz on a Mac) to reduce frustrating delays. Investing in a 17″ screen (or bigger) is also a good idea if you're going to be doing a lot of design work.

You have to be honest with yourself: if after a few weeks or months of experimenting with the software your results still look amateurish, or lack the functionality you require, then your site is never going to make you rich unless you get professional help.

Beyond the basics

There are certain things you want any site to achieve: it must have compelling content, it must download quickly and it must be easy to use. Taking each of these objectives in turn, will take you through the process of improving your site to professional standards. The links at the end of the chapter will provide you with more details.

Content

It's amazing how poor much of the content on the web is. Thoughtlessness is the major reason for illogical navigation and self-indulgent, inaccurate and badly written text ... which means it's actually pretty easy for someone with relatively little experience to get a head start on the competition if they just pay attention to the details. Always keep in mind how a user will approach your site, and shower your home page with love and affection. Does your home page tell users what your site does at a glance? If you sell shoes does it tell them that you have the best shoes at the best prices? If you offer news does it tell them that you have the best journalists updating the site constantly with exclusive stories? Make sure it does a fantastic sales job and then ask yourself how easy it is to then find what you want on the site. Surf it yourself and be as critical as possible – check that your spelling and grammar are accurate and make sure there are no broken links. Check you don't have reams of text that no one can be bothered to read – if you find it boring your users are going to be clicking away very quickly. Make sure you can navigate your way round the site easily.

There are many ways to enhance your content for free. There are places on the web where you can download interactive quizzes, get search engines that will search your site, get news wires or chat rooms and message boards for free. There are also clip art sites that have artwork you can download for free, from 'submit' buttons to cartoons. (You'll find a list at the end of the chapter.)

Always keep in mind how a user will approach your site, and shower your home page with love and affection.

Download speed

A favourite quote among web designers is that most users won't wait more than eight seconds for a page to download. Since very few pages download this quickly – even on sites with huge traffic like Yahoo! and the BBC – this quite clearly isn't the case. But beyond 20 seconds and your reader's finger is starting to get itchy over the mouse; 30 seconds and you've probably lost them. The way to make pages download quickly – and this is most important with your home page – is to keep it simple. Image files – usually GIFs or JPEGs – take longer the bigger they are, so keep graphics small and to a minimum. There are several sites (listed below) that will help your site perform better by spidering your site for coding errors or singling out large and inefficient images (there are nifty bits of software they can direct you to that will make your files more efficient, and therefore faster loading).

Animation – whether using a program like Flash or something simpler like GIFbuilder – almost always takes a long time to load so keep it to a minimum, especially on your home page (unless of course you intend to have more of a 'cover' for your site which is really just to show off – in which case do just that!). Frames also tend to slow down pages and as they are pretty ugly and often unreadable by search engines (see Chapter 7 on marketing) it's a good idea to avoid them.

The other thing that can vastly affect the download

speed of your site is the sort of server you're on (see Hosting below).

Easy to use

The web is a frustrating place for users. Search engines rarely produce the results they promise and sites are often so Byzantine in their structure that it's impossible to find what you want. If you start with the assumption that no one who comes to your site has ever been online before this should help you to keep your site simple. Whether or not you are selling goods, think of your site like a big department store. As soon as you walk in the door you should get some idea from the design and ambience what sort of store it is. You know instantly whether you're in Harvey Nichols or Kwik Save, and this is something you must consider when building your site - do the colours, typefaces and images give the right impression?

Once inside the store you start looking for signs like 'lingerie' or 'menswear' that you know will take you straight to the department you're after. So make sure your site makes it easy for users to find their way around. Also, make sure users can then get from Menswear to Lingerie without having to go up six flights of stairs and getting lost twice!

Using the internet still isn't second nature for the vast majority of your potential customers so make sure you take care of them. If you're going to sell something ensure they can check out delivery costs and your returns policy before they've handed over their credit card details. Even some of the big e-commerce sites don't make it easy to access this kind of information – and it's impossible to know how many potential customers they're putting off because of it.

Another tip is never to underestimate the stupidity of the surfing public. Never assume your users know what your site is about. If you update the site every day – tell them! If you have a particular mission – put your mission statement clearly on the site. The words 'click here' are the most powerful command in the English language right now. Don't assume people will intuitively know that an image or graphic is a link if you don't tell them. Put signposts everywhere and don't rely on people using their browser's back button to get themselves around.

The words 'click here' are the most powerful command in the English language right now.

E-commerce

It's a myth that you can't build an e-commerce site yourself, but you will need additional software and pay to be on a secure server (see Hosting below). Actinic (*www.actinic.com*) has e-commerce software specifically designed for small businesses. Shop@ssistant is another affordable option for the DIY e-commerce entrepreneur and Net Store (*www.net-store.com*) still costs less than £500. You can also use outside sites to manage credit card transactions for you. Companies like Netbanx, Secure

Trading and NatWest's Streamline will manage credit card transactions for you for a fee between (usually) 2–9 per cent. These sites will often handle the validation and some of the accounting for you. They will also communicate with your credit card merchant.

A merchant is a credit card company like Visa, Mastercard or Amex (there is a list of phone numbers in the directory) and you will have to register with these companies to accept payment from their cardholders. As they are taking a risk that you won't deliver your goods they charge what is known as a Merchant Service Charge which can be anything up to 15 per cent on the purchase price.

Your domain name

Your site will need a URL (a Uniform Resource Locator). This is also called your domain name, which to most people is just the address (ending in *.com*, *.co.uk*, *.net* etc.) they type in to be taken to your site. Each country has an official registry of names to make sure that no two people can use the same domain at the same time. If you want to be taken seriously you are going to need a domain name that's easy to remember. It's worth spending hours, days or even weeks to get a good domain for your site – and it will probably take weeks because you can bet that whenever you come up with a good name, someone else will already be using it.

To find out if the domain name you want is available try sites like *netnames.com* and *uk2.net*. Registering a *.co.uk* is free at sites like *freenetnames.co.uk*, but there is a catch (you usually have to have your site hosted – see below – with them for a fixed period). There are restrictions on registering certain suffixes like *.org*, *.gov* and any foreign domains (Italy's *.it* and Tonga's *.to* are popular choices) but these are simply explained when you try to register.

If the name you want is already in use there's not a lot you can do about it. There has been a frenzy of 'cyber squatting' in the past year where opportunists have made use of free and cheap registrations and snapped up loads of good names in the hope that someone like you will come along and offer them a fortune for a certain name. It's worth registering with *www.unclaimeddomains.com* as many of these cyber squatters fail to keep up the rent on these names – you have to pay rent every two years to hang on to your domain – and you can pick them up for less than their extortionate ransom.

If you have an unusual company name and you can prove that someone has registered that name with the sole intention of extorting money from you, then this is illegal and there are several cases of cyber squatters being sued for their opportunism.

There are several rules to observe when deciding on a domain name for your company:

1. Make sure it's easy to spell. The last thing you want is for users not to be able to find your site because they couldn't spell your URL.

2. Keep it as short as possible. The longer the URL, the greater the chance that someone will hit the wrong key and never find your site. It's also harder to remember longer domain names.

3. Ask yourself if it conveys the right image. Domain names usually do one of two things – they either tell users exactly what you do (e.g. *www.weselltoiletpaper. com*) or they help you create a brand (e.g. *www.wipe. com*). Think about what you want your domain name to say about your company.

4. If at all possible, try to register an international suffix like *.com* or *.net*. Being a *.co.uk* won't help you be taken seriously if you intend to expand abroad.

5. Avoid hyphens. Some people like hyphens because words look better written down if they're separated, but users often forget about them. If at all possible, register your domain without a hyphen, with it, and with a range of suffixes that you can redirect to the same site.

NB: If you get a third party to register your domain for you (e.g. your ISP [Internet Service Provider] or a design agency) make sure that you own the URL. There have been reports of unscrupulous agencies and ISPs registering domains in their company name and then preventing clients ditching them in the future. You should also be aware that the address and phone number you give when you register the domain may be listed in the domain 'Who Is' information. If you give your home address and phone number it's possible that you might get the odd phone call or letter you really don't want to receive.

Hosting

Once your site has been built and you have a domain name, you have to upload it on to a server – basically a powerful computer – that enables users to visit your site. If you've never been involved with the internet before, the concept of hosting is quite a weird one to get your head round, but it's actually not that hard to understand. Hosting simply means that a server has your site taking up some of its memory. If yours is a small site you will almost certainly share a server with several other sites. You will be given a code – effectively a password – which gives you access to this server via your modem to upload information to it through an FTP (File Transfer Protocol) program. This may sound complicated, but once you're set up, uploading is as simple as a click of the mouse. Your site will also be given a code (an Internet Protocol address) which corresponds to your unique URL. You don't have to be geographically near your host and up and down the country there are companies which provide hosting. Most ISPs offer some sort of free web space as part of their service but there are also specialist hosting services. Check with your ISP what kind of service they offer, but the chances are that there will be limitations on the domain names you can use (i.e. the letters 'aol' or 'demon' may appear in your URL) and the size of site they will host.

When you approach a company to do your hosting (*Internet Works* magazine publishes a monthly league table on which company is currently performing the best) don't expect them to give a damn what your site is about. They will just want to know how much web space you need and what your email requirements are.

Web space is measured in megabytes. As a rough guide, 100 pages of text is about 10Mb. The more graphics, animation etc you have on your site, the more web space you will need. If you use a design program like Dreamweaver it will tell you how many 'megs' your site is. Hosting companies will also charge you for delivering email and this can vary depending what sort of email service you want. The cheapest is usually SMTP (Simple Mail Transport Protocol) delivery which simply redirects your email to your current account with your ISP. You can then change the identity preferences in your email software to make it look like your mail is being delivered from your domain. There are also POP3 (Post Office Protocol) accounts which set up a mailbox just for your domain which you access directly. Discuss your requirements with your host and get a range of quotes.

There are often bandwidth restrictions on shared servers which prevent too many people accessing your site at any one time and therefore crowding out access to another site. Even if your site is quite small in terms of megabytes, if you expect huge quantities of traffic you want to make sure that your server can cope. And if you are going to accept credit card details on your site, you will need to make sure that your site is held on a secure server; your ISP or host will discuss this with you. It should be possible to get a small site hosted for around £35 a month + VAT. Email accounts could add another £15 or so, but don't just go with the cheapest quote – choose a company with a good technical support phone line (not just via email) and one that will guarantee to move your site to a different server if you get more traffic.

You also need to ensure that your host gives you FTP access to your site. This will enable you to make changes to your site's content with greater control than sites you can only update via a browser.

Keep in mind that it is really important that you find a good host who puts you on a good server. Being on a crowded server can mean your site downloads slowly and prevents more than a couple of people looking at your site at any one time. The difference in download speeds between servers is quite shocking.

Instructing a web designer

As a general rule, you should try and find a designer the

same way you would a plumber – get a personal recommendation. If you see a site you like, send an email to the webmaster and ask who designed it. Get the URL of the design company and see if there are URLs of other sites they've built. Then contact their clients and see if they're happy with the work that's been done.

Most net magazines are full of ads for design companies willing to take on all sorts of work. Some will charge by the page and some will charge hundreds of thousands – even millions – of pounds for helping you to plan and execute an entire online strategy. Finding the right company to do the work will take research both in terms of finding the right partner, and in knowing exactly what kind of site you want them to build.

A decent web design agency will do everything from registering your domain name, to sorting out your hosting requirements to actually designing the site itself. But they should also provide services like registering your site with search engines (you'll find more detail on this in Chapter 7) which means making sure that the META tags – a special code some search engines use to work out what your site is about – and your page descriptions correspond with the content of your site. Sometimes you hear horror stories about design companies cutting corners – like the agency that designed an entertainment listings site on a template they had previously used for a car mechanic's site – which meant the search engines listed the entertainment site under 'car dealerships'!

You need to find a designer that will take the time to make sure your site downloads fast and navigates easily – don't assume that because they are professionals they will take the same amount of care that you would if only you knew how to. If your site needs regular updating, you might also need some training from your design agency so that you can maintain the site in-house.

Because design is such a crucial part of any site's success, it's important that you develop a good relationship with your design company. Sometimes it's worth making them a partner in your business. Samir Satchu, who runs the London Underground community site *tubehell.com*, actually made his design company stakeholders in his business: 'Getting Kerb [the design agency] onboard was crucial to me,' says the entrepreneur. 'I didn't have the money when I was starting out to pay them so paying them with equity was the best deal for both of us. I've got a talented design team who are committed to me because they have a stake in my success. They do well out of it too as hopefully their share in the company will be worth more than any fee they could have charged me.'

Some agencies – especially the new ones – can't afford to work for equity alone as they have bills to meet before you reach the giddy heights of the stock exchange. Others are suspicious that if your idea isn't good enough to have got investors queuing up then it's too big a risk for them. It can be difficult to get a good deal but if you work out exactly what you want and speak to as many agencies as possible, you should find yourself at the start of a beautiful friendship.

Even if you only have a budget of a few hundred pounds, you should still be able to find a company to take on your project, but you need to have realistic expectations that you're not going to get a racehorse for the price of a Blackpool donkey.

You need to have realistic expectations that you're not going to get a racehorse for the price of a Blackpool donkey.

Designer checklist

If you can get satisfactory answers to the following questions, then you can feel reasonably confident about commissioning a designer to start work:

1. Can I see your portfolio and speak to previous clients?

2. Why do you want to take on my project? (You should try and find a designer who's enthusiastic about your product and understands your market.)

3. What do you need from me? (Make sure you understand what your commitment to them will be besides the money. Do you need to attend endless meetings, provide them with logos, photos and text?)

4. What are your payment terms? (These vary enormously but you need to establish when you will hand over the money. Expect to pay a deposit. Also check to see if

there are any hidden ongoing costs (usually associated with hosting).)

5. Will they help you maintain your site? (Find out if they can train you to maintain your site or how much they will charge you to make updates on your behalf.)

Once your site is built, you should be able to agree with all the following statements:

The design of my site creates the right impression. ☐

My site is easy to navigate. ☐

My home page downloads in less than 20 seconds. ☐

My site is hosted on a good server by a company offering comprehensive technical support. ☐

I am happy with my relationship with my designer. ☐

Directory

Domain name registration

http://www.site-registrations.co.uk/index.html
Also sells domains for some European countries

http://www.allukdomains.co.uk/
http://www.magic-moments.com
Comprehensive international search available – including .to (Tonga) and .it (Italy)

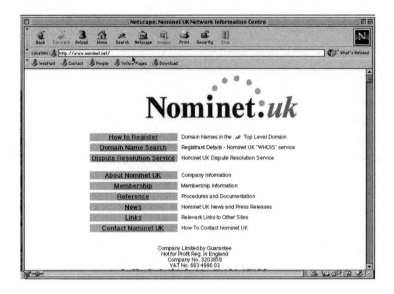

http://www.nominet.net/

Most famous but not the cheapest

http://www.safenames.com/

Offers international domain names

http://uk2.net/

Claims to be the cheapest registration service for all the main domains

Hosting services

Listed in no particular order, these companies offer professional hosting options:

www.u-net.net
www.cix.co.uk
www.clara.net
www.dircon.net
www.magic-moments.com
www.rapidsite.co.uk
www.datagate.co.uk
www.netdirect.net.uk
www.cableinet.co.uk
www.enterprise.net

Internet Service Providers

http://www.webpromotion.co.uk/isps.htm
List of links to ISPs

http://www.iwks.com/isplist/list.htm
A comprehensive list of ISPs from *Internet Works* magazine

DIY Web design

http://www.netmag.co.uk/webbuilder/default.asp
Lots of basic and some more advanced stuff from *.net* magazine

http://www.freenetname.co.uk/tutorial/default.asp

Work through the basics here

http://development.alpha-project.net/

Easy to follow web tutorials

http://resources.hitbox.com/

Major directory of resources for webmasters

http://www.tips-tricks.com

Step-by-step guide to site building

http://www.tips-tricks.com/web_tools.shtml
Comprehensive list of web page editors with links to manufacturers' sites

http://www.beyondcomputingmag.com/Notices/neyeopen2.html
Website design tips

http://hotwired.lycos.com/webmonkey/design/site_building/
All the gen on web design from a bunch of real techies at Webmonkey

http://netb2b.com/educational_tracks/
Articles on web design and content management

http://www.internet.com/sections/webdev.html
Links to more technically advanced programmers' sites

Free tools

http://www.beseen.com/
Use free beseen (they carry their own advertising to pay for the service) quizzes, bulletin boards and search engines

http://www.bravenet.com
Loads of free stuff from site-specific search engines to message boards

http://www.gsponline.com/free/index.html
Everything from chat rooms to CGI (Common Gateway Interface) scripts

http://www.freewebtemplates.com

Free graphics, clip art etc and web design tutorials – you can even get JavaScript written for you

http://development.alpha-project.net/

Photos, templates and wallpaper to use on your site

http://www.siteinspector.com

Checks your site for errors

http://www.websitegarage.com

Runs diagnostic tests on your site – coding, image size, even spelling!

http://www.gifcruncher.com
http://www.jpegcruncher.com

Optimises your images for the web for fast downloading

http://positionagent.linkexchange.com

Free check on your search engine rating

http://www.searchenginewatch.com/

Tips on improving your ranking on search engines

http://www.escriptzone.com

Lots of free scripts to add counters, dates etc. to your pages

http://JavaScriptSource.com

Hundreds of free JavaScripts to download to liven up your pages – from animation to games

http://reallybig.com/devcom.shtml
Resources for web builders including clip art and Java programs

http://www.thefreesite.com
Major directory of links to tons of free stuff from graphics to web space

http://vicinities.com
Free forum and networking services

http://resources.hitbox.com/
Polls, stats, HTML code tester, image file size reducer

http://apps3.vantagenet.com/site/horoscope.asp
Get a free horoscope on your site!

Free downloads

http://www.macromedia.com/software/downloads/
Free trial versions of design software Dreamweaver, Director, Fireworks, Flash and Freehand to download

http://www.adobe.com/products/tryadobe/main.html
Save-disabled versions of all Adobe's applications

http://www.microsoft.com/downloads/
Some decent freebies – mainly extra bits to add to your current programs

http://www.netmag.co.uk/software/default.asp
Free software from .net magazine including HTML tools and file
transfer clients (used for uploading your pages)

http://www.zdnet.com/downloads/
Searchable database of freeware/shareware for all operating
systems

http://filefarm.internet.com/filefarm/
Free downloadable demos for every operating system including
graphics and the latest versions of browsers

http://download.cnet.com/
Free downloads of demo versions and shareware

http://tucows.mirror.ac.uk/
Comprehensive free download site – this is a local UK version
for faster download

http://ukms.mac.tucows.com/
And a local site for Macs

E-commerce

E-commerce software can be downloaded at these sites:

http://www.actinic.co.uk
http://www.floyd.co.uk
http://www.cows.co.uk

http://www.jshop.co.uk
http://www.erol.co.uk
http://www.intershop.co.uk

The following sites can arrange for your credit card payments to be processed:

http://www.netbanx.com
http://www.worldpay.com
http://www.datacash.com
http://www.secpay.com
http://www.securetrading.com

Merchants

Barclays: tel 0800 616161
HSBC: tel 0345 023344
Bank of Scotland: tel 01223 845594
Natwest Streamline: tel 0800 010166

Logistics

These companies can take care of your deliveries:

http://www.royalmail.co.uk
http://www.dhl.co.uk
http:// www.fedex.com/gb
http://www.ups.com
http://www.unitedcarriersgroup.co.uk
http://www.businessexpress.co.uk
http://www.tnt.co.uk

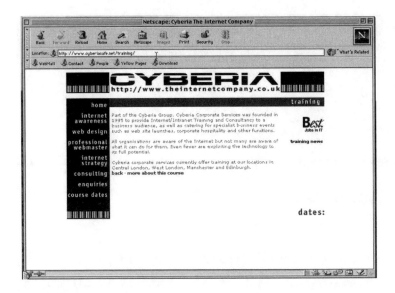

Training

http://www.cyberiacafe.net/training
Courses available throughout the year in London, Manchester and Edinburgh from the Cyberia Cafe people

http://www.bicentre.co.uk
Birmingham training centre

http://www.trainingpages.co.uk
A searchable database of courses available in the UK for business and IT training needs, from Photoshop and Dreamweaver to marketing and financial management

Entrepreneur Profile   Samir Satchu

1.   Name
Samir Satchu

2.   Age
27

3   URL of your business
www.tubehell.com

4.   What is the purpose/nature of your business/website?
A virtual community service for Tubehellers – one million daily Tube users in particular – delivering personalised Tube news over the internet.

5.   Date your business started
Launched 7 December 1999.

6.   Is this your first new media venture?
Yes.

7.   Briefly describe your previous business experience and state how useful this was in starting your site.
Worked briefly as a corporate lawyer and then in an internet-only

investment bank raising money for pre-IPO internet/new media companies. Useful to see how things worked from the capital-raising side – what VCs are looking for etc. In terms of learning about managing something successfully on a day-to-day, operational level, there is no substitute for actual experience.

8. Briefly outline your educational qualifications. Please state which universities/colleges you got these qualifications from.

Trinity College, Cambridge BA(Hons) First Class – History 1994, Harvard Law School, Juris Doctor, 1998.

9. Were you able to/did you try to raise seed financing from family and friends? If so, how much did you raise.

Yes – £200,000.

10. Did you have any useful contacts when it came to raising finance? If so, what kind of introductions proved to be the most useful?

Your network is your most important ally – certainly introductions/ contacts will get you into meetings that you might not have got into through a cold call.

11. Roughly how much money did you raise in venture capital and was this enough?

Looking to raise £1.5-2 million.

12. How many people were there on your management team?

Currently two, this needs to be bolstered up significantly.

13. How useful have you found networking events like First Tuesday and BoobNight?

Generally try to avoid.

14. What would you do differently if you had to start all over again?

Draw up more rigorous contracts with partner companies, sort out a good hosting service from the outset.

15. What do you think are the criteria that have most helped you make a success of your business (e.g. having first mover advantage, a brilliant marketing campaign, bloody-mindedness)?

Bringing something slightly different to the market, great timing at launch, great PR and marketing, although the product can PR and market itself pretty well anyway, and a realisation that nothing will work without hard work.

16. What's been the hardest thing you've had to face since starting your business?

Finding decent people, companies who can actually deliver against their promises and contractual obligations.

17. What's the most useful piece of advice you've been given?

It won't happen without hard work.

18. What's the one piece of advice you wish someone had given you, but didn't?

Trust very few people.

19. Do you believe it's still possible for someone with only a good idea and determination to succeed in new media – or is it all about raising money these days?

Less and less so unless they have a background of delivering something from scratch or are experienced managers or are suitably well connected to get some token celebrity to sit on their board.

20. Are you in profit?

Errm ... no.

4 Profit and progress

A work in progress

ESSENTIALLY, MOST INTERNET SITES ARE simply virtual versions of real world businesses. They operate in similar ways to conventional businesses and have the same sources of income – advertising, subscriptions, commissions etc. But there are two ways in which e-businesses operate in an entirely different way from real world offerings.

It's almost too obvious to say, but in the online arena you are only one click away from the competition. If you give bad service in a high street shop you still stand a chance of getting repeat business from that customer just because to visit a rival entails three buses and a train trip in the wrong direction. On the internet you can lose your customers forever for just the tiniest error. And the chances are you won't lose just one customer, you'll lose the lot, since email, chat rooms, message boards and newsgroups can spread news of bad service at speeds greater than 56kbps. Equally, if you treat one customer well, good word of mouth on the internet can bring many more customers your way.

The other way in which online businesses operate in an arena of their own is that your users can - and will - tell you exactly what they think of your service. This gives online businesses the biggest advantage over their real world counterparts and is something you must use to your advantage.

Whether or not your customers or users send you emails suggesting improvements to your service, they still tell you everything you need to know about improving your site. If you thought you could take a breather now that your site is up and running, think again.

In the online arena you are only one click away from the competition. On the internet you can lose your customers forever for just the tiniest error

Analysing your stats

The biggest advantage online businesses have over real world businesses is the tracking statistics or user logs. These should be provided by your host and will tell you how many people have visited your site and when. They will tell you which pages are your most popular and how people reached your site. In addition to the statistics provided by your host, you can also get more info on your

Stats are God's little gift to internet entrepreneurs and if you learn to interpret them they will guide you down a path paved with gold.

users by using a range of stat tracking services. Sites like *www.hitbox.com* and *www.stattrack.com* offer free stats services in exchange for putting their logo somewhere discreetly on your site. Stats are God's little gift to internet entrepreneurs and if you learn to interpret them they will guide you down a path paved with gold.

Depending on what stat software you use, you will be able to determine the most useful array of information on your users. You will find out what domain name they came from. If most of your users are private individuals using Freeserve or AOL accounts this might not be quite so valuable. But if you have a business-to-business (B2B) site and you can tell that visitors have come from companyxyz.com then this can help you figure out who is not getting your message, who's checking you out and who can't get enough of you. If you can tell that a certain sector of your target audience is missing, then this will help you save time and money marketing to get their business.

Your stats will tell you what time of day your visitors come, what part of the world they come from and which site directed their attention your way. Stats will also tell you how people move around your site and identify which are your most popular pages. Use this information to promote certain pages more heavily or produce more content of a certain sort to capitalise on interest in your most popular elements. And if you know that some pages are more popular than others, then make sure advertising space on those pages sells for a premium.

If yours is an e-commerce site, you can also easily monitor what's selling and quickly order more of the same.

Feedback

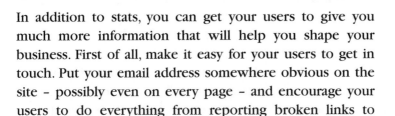

In addition to stats, you can get your users to give you much more information that will help you shape your business. First of all, make it easy for your users to get in touch. Put your email address somewhere obvious on the site – possibly even on every page – and encourage your users to do everything from reporting broken links to suggesting new products to sell.

The community aspect of the web has often been over-sold, but email and other elements allow users to develop a sense of membership to a website that they would never feel for a shop or magazine. Users expect to be able to inter-act if they want to and there are elements you can intro-duce into your site to solicit as much feedback as possible.

The first thing you should do is create a mailing list for users to join. This can be so you can alert them to special offers, send them newsflashes or alert them to improve-ments in your site. Your host or your design agency should be able to provide you with a script that allows you to have a form on your site for readers to fill in and provide information about themselves. If you ask for too much information (like their home phone numbers or salary) you might put people off joining. Keep it simple: name, email address and occupation should be enough. If it's appropriate, ask them what products or services they'd most like to receive information about. Always ask them how they found out about your site as this is vital to assess the effectiveness of your marketing campaigns.

Some sites require users to register before they are able to access the full service, rather than making it voluntary to sign up. If your business relies on advertising income, then the more detail you can give advertisers about your readers the better. But be warned, compulsory registration gets up people's noses and many will click away immediately.

Another good way of getting information about your users – and therefore information to help you maximise your profits – is to introduce message boards and chat rooms into your service. Again, these services are available for free (you might have to have compulsory advertising or someone else's logo on these pages) or your designer can integrate them into the site for you. Message boards allow your users to speak to each other and help create a sense of community. They also provide you with detailed information about their habits or the gaps in their knowledge that your site can fill. If you run a gardening site and lots of messages get left asking for tips about topsoil, then you know that (a) you should provide that information yourself and (b) you should be talking to topsoil distributors about advertising on your site.

Profit drivers

Once your site has been active for a few months, you should start to build a picture of where future revenue is likely to come from. If you can interpret the information your users give you and use that information to accurately predict the immediate future, this will give you a serious advantage in your quest to turn a profit. Let's take the four main revenue sources - advertising, subscription, affiliate marketing and retail - in turn.

Advertising

The first thing an advertiser will want to know about your site is how many people visit it. You have probably heard of sites claiming to have 250,000 hits a week, but hits are not visitors. Every item on the screen - an image, link or block of text - registers a hit. So a user might call up one page and register 20 hits. For this reason it's been a long time since advertisers have asked you how many 'hits' you're getting. A far more accurate measurement of traffic is the 'page impression' and your stats will tell you how many requests for pages are made every day, week and month. Other advertisers like to compare like for like: if they're used to advertising in print publications that can categorically say they have 10,000 readers, an advertiser might want to know how many 'unique visitors' you have.

Once you start to build a picture of who is visiting your site (and how many, of course) you can start to target advertisers more effectively. Think about companies who would also want to reach your readership.

Selling advertising space for websites can be a very tough job and you have to use every iota of information you have to make a sale. Think creatively and laterally about who potential advertisers might be and also think about the opportunities your site can offer advertisers. Maybe they can sponsor a certain section or you could build a micro site (usually a two to four page site with lots of information about your advertisers' services) for them to enhance the value of advertising with you instead of a widely-read print rival.

Use your stats to wow advertisers

Use your stats to wow advertisers. Demonstrate to them that you can deliver their target audience. That audience might be smaller than another site's or another publication's, but if you can prove that you target a certain niche better than anyone else you can still persuade people to advertise on your site. You will find it easier to attract advertising if you have a cool brand that other companies want to rub off on them – don't just sell them figures, sell them a dream! If your page impressions start to top 50,000 a month you can register with one of the sales agencies to be an affiliate. *www.doublecheck.net*, *www.247media.com* and *www.flycast.com* all sell advertising on behalf of website publishers on a page impression basis. They won't bring you in a huge income – possibly just a few hundred pounds if your traffic stays low – but it's better than a poke in the eye! You should also register your site with the Directory of Media Owners (*www.domo.co.uk*) so planning and buying agencies can find out about you.

Subscription

If users have been registering their details with you in droves and you are damn sure of their appetite and need for your service, you may have a case for charging a subscription. Generally, surfers like the web to be free and the only successful subscription sites tend to be financial sites offering real-time share information. Magazines that have tried to put their content online and charge people for access have generally had to make access free sooner or later. If your site offers exclusive information that readers could potentially profit from (i.e. you give them access to new customers, clients or revenue streams) then you might also be able to successfully charge a subscription. If it's the general public you want to use your site, don't even think about charging for access.

Keep in mind that if someone has paid a subscription they don't then expect to be

Surfers like the web to be free and the only successful subscription sites tend to be financial sites offering real-time share information.

If it's the general public you want to use your site, don't even think about charging for access.

bombarded by advertising messages. And while advertisers might like the extra information you can ask for from subscribers, they know that a subscription charge is a barrier to exponential growth. If you can work your way to profit without charging for it, then this is a wise way to move ahead.

Affiliate marketing

Once upon a time, the clever boys and girls at Amazon came up with a brilliant way to increase sales and brand awareness: affiliate marketing. It works like this: you put an ad for Amazon on your site (the artwork is free and quick to download from their site) and if one of your readers clicks on it – and then buys something from Amazon – you get between five and 15 per cent of the value of the sale. There are now hundreds of affiliate schemes available to websites selling everything from CDs to printer cartridges to chrome plated nutcrackers (you'll find a list of them in the directory at the end of the chapter), and they all work in pretty much the same way.

Opinion on their usefulness varies. On the one hand it costs you nothing and could bring you an income, but as most of the goods sold cost under £10, you need a lot of five per cents to get to the £30 minimum you need to earn before you are sent a cheque. You are in effect giving lots of cheap advertising to affiliate scheme operators. On the other hand, the banners and buttons they make available can make your site look more professional and like the sort of site people want to advertise on and take seriously.

It is possible to set up your own version of an affiliate scheme which stands a better chance of bringing you in more money. If your site has a high number of cooks visiting it, perhaps you could do a deal with a pan or utensil manufacturer to help shift their stock in exchange for a 25 per cent to 50 per cent cut. This might sound a lot – but it's less than a manufacturer would give to a retailer and saves them on all sorts of distribution and marketing costs. If your stats – and information you've gathered from message boards and chat rooms – prove that you're hitting their target market they have nothing to lose by agreeing to such terms. If you can negotiate to be their exclusive online partner, then that's even better.

Retail

Just as a high street retailer keeps a close eye on what's selling, so must you if you run an e-commerce site. If you see that certain products shift fast, then order more of them, or more similar products. Let readers tell you exactly what they would like you to sell – and if you get enough requests, order in the stock.

Always visit your rivals' sites to make sure your prices are competitive as it's much easier to do price comparisons online than it is on the high street. If you can't compete on price, make sure your users know that you compete on service and reliability.

Really examine your stats against your purchases. If you know that hundreds of people have visited a certain page with a certain product on it but haven't bought it, try to work out why. It might just be that a broken link stopped users moving to the virtual checkout, or it might be that you've used a poor quality photo of a product or are charging too much. Even if users don't become customers, their browsing habits can still tell you everything you need to know about the sorts of products they are interested in buying.

 ## Staying flexible

You may have worked your fingers to the bone getting your site up and running, but you must be prepared to recognise its flaws. Let your stats and feedback information guide you to move pages around, experiment with layout and navigation as well as content. A site that doesn't respond to the information freely available to it will wither and die.

A site that doesn't respond to the information freely available to it will wither and die.

If you're not getting the feedback you wanted or you just can't quite work out why visitors aren't using the site in the way you expected, then why not introduce a formal questionnaire into your service. Explain that it only takes five minutes to answer and helps you keep costs down (and therefore your service remains free). There are several web marketing companies (like *www.netpoll.net*) that can help you conduct all sorts of research including questionnaires and focus groups.

There are really only two questions worth asking yourself at this point:

Do I understand what my users want from me? ☐

Am I giving it to them? ☐

Directory

These sites offer suggestions for increasing your revenue. They include affiliate schemes, tips on selling more advertising and links to professional advisers.

http://www.webpromotion.co.uk/adnetworks.htm
List of links to the leading advertising agencies on the web – the people who sell your ad space for you

http://www.webpromotion.co.uk/affiliateprograms.htm
Learn how to set up your own affiliate scheme

http://www.associateprograms.com
Lots of affiliate schemes to join

http://www.associate-it.com
More examples of affiliates (also known as associate schemes)

http://216.147.78.147/directory/associate.html
Links to lists of dozens of schemes

http://www.refer-it.com
Add your own affiliate scheme to a network

http://www.bizweb2000.com
Links to sites that help set up your own affiliate scheme

E-commerce

http://sellitontheweb.com
Tips and how-to guides on setting up an e-commerce site

http://ecommerce.internet.com
Loads of info on the e-commerce side of your business

http://www.internetwk.com/service
Advice on good customer service practices

Statistics and tracking services

http://www.webtrends.com
Professional stat solutions. Trial versions available to download

http://www.activeconcepts.com
More programs to buy. Download trial versions to use on all platforms

http://www.stattrack.com
Free statistical analysis in return for a button on your site

http://www.hitbox.com
Thoroughly comprehensive free analysis in return for a button or a banner

http://www.tech-sol.net/interlinks/counters.htm
List of free counters and statistics programs/services

Entrepreneur Profile | Steve Gandy

1. Name
Steve Gandy

2. Age
39

3. URL of your business
www.quip.co.uk

4. What is the purpose/nature of your business/website?
E-telco (cheap telephone calls service registered for via the web).

5. Date your business started
Incorporated 25 June 1999; first trading 15 January 2000.

6. Is this your first new media venture?
Yes.

7. Briefly describe your previous business experience and state how useful this was in starting your site.
Involved in business start-up as a junior employee (which failed – very good learning!). Set up business as wholly owned subsidiary of BT – this was successful – again great learning.

8. Briefly outline your educational qualifications. Please state which universities/colleges you got these qualifications from.

BA(Hons) in Business Studies from the University of Sheffield.

9. Were you able to/did you try to raise seed financing from family and friends? If so, how much did you raise?

No.

10. Did you have any useful contacts when it came to raising finance? If so, what kind of introductions proved to be the most useful?

Those from people who had already been through seed and mezzanine rounds.

11. Roughly how much money did you raise in venture capital and was this enough?

We're now doing second round as first round didn't provide sufficient marketing money.

12. How many people were there on your management team?

Six.

13. How useful have you found networking events like First Tuesday and BoobNight?

Limited.

14. What would you do differently if you had to start all over again?

Ask for more money!

15. What do you think are the criteria that have most helped you make a success of your business (e.g. having first mover advantage, a brilliant marketing campaign, bloody-mindedness)?

All of the above, especially tenacity. Vision is important and so is attention to the detail that affects customers – getting close to customers via the web is difficult.

16. What's been the hardest thing you've had to face since starting your business?

Fitting stuff into a 24 hour day. Managing the shareholders' expectations.

17. What's the most useful piece of advice you've been given?

Select the very best agency support you can afford (across all areas of business advice).

18. What's the one piece of advice you wish someone had given you, but didn't?

Ask for more marketing money.

19. Do you believe it's still possible for someone with only a good idea and determination to succeed in new media – or is it all about raising money these days?

If there is a genuine unique proposition with sufficiently wide appeal, yes. Me-too's won't cut it.

20. Are you in profit?

No, but I will be!

5 Preparing your business plan

IF YOU'VE NEVER BEEN IN business before, it's quite possible you've never seen a business plan and have no idea why they're important, or know how to write one. Generally, business plans have two objectives: to help the management team plan the growth of the company and to raise finance. Management consultancy Deloitte and Touche's website has this neat description of a business plan in its online help pack:

Business plans have two objectives: to help the management team plan the growth of the company and to raise finance.

'The business plan is really a document that conveys a company's exciting prospects and growth potential, and thereby sells the business to potential backers.

These backers include the management team as well as potential lenders and investors. The business plan can thus be used to attract support both from within and from outside the company.'

In the current climate it is almost impossible for an Internet company to make its mark without serious financial backing, so you'll almost certainly need a business plan that's capable of demonstrating your potential to investors. The trend seems to be for shorter business plans (20–25 pages, or less) to secure investment, but if you're jumping through hoops anyway, producing a slightly longer operational business plan for internal use might be a wise document to produce at this stage.

Most investors want you to write your plan yourself although this is typically a service provided by external management consultants, incubators and other individuals who can help you raise finance. The theory is that investors can spot consultants' jargon and tricks and may discount such a plan as insincere. Anyway, if you write it yourself (or at least have a heavy hand in its creation) you will understand your business much better.

Writing something as official as a business plan can be daunting for many entrepreneurs who think guts alone will lead to glory. Compared to the ducking and diving of business, sitting down to methodically write a plan is extremely dull. These are the most common reasons for avoiding writing a business plan, but if you take the time to write one properly, your business plan will be a virtual business adviser that will guide you through the coming months. In addition to the advice here, there are umpteen sites that will take you through writing business plans (refer to directory at the end of the chapter) that show you sample plans to reassure you that you're on the right track. Don't be intimidated: take your time and do it thoroughly. No matter how unconventional your business, there are certain standard criteria an investor will want to see in your business plan which are usually set out in the following structure:

1. An executive summary (essentially a condensed version of the full business plan).

2. A description and history of the company.

3. An analysis of the market and the competition.

4. An analysis of revenue streams.

5. A marketing plan.

6. An operating plan.

7. Financial forecasts and data.

8. Appendices (the management team's CVs, organisational structure and financial data, usually graphically presented).

The two most important parts of a business plan are the executive summary and the CVs of the management team.

According to most investors looking at internet companies, the two most important parts of a business plan are the executive summary and the CVs of the management team. There is no point in lying just to get an investor to meet with you. No one is going to give you money without a thorough investigation into the claims you make. If you lie you will be found out. Equally, you may feel that there is no way you can accurately predict your company's future, but if you can make a convincing case for your best case scenario, this is certainly acceptable. Some of the daydreaming and fanciful brainstorming you'll do in preparing your business plan is important in enlarging your ambitions to help you see the full potential of your business.

'There are lies, damned lies and business plans.' This comes from one entrepreneur who didn't want their name attributed with such a quote. 'I really couldn't believe some of the stuff that went into our business plan at first. It seemed utterly incredible that me and my mates were going to achieve a tenth of what we put on paper. But the simple process of writing it in black and white – and then forcing ourselves to plot a likely route to those fanciful ends – really, really helped us. It definitely gave us something to aim for.'

> 'There are lies, damned lies and business plans.'

Although venture capitalists (VCs), business angels and other investors see hundreds of business plans a month the general consensus is that it is of no value whatsoever to make your business plan try to stand out from the pile in their in-trays. Just print it soberly on white A4 paper and bind it with a staple or a paper clip. Don't send it on a CD-ROM or on shiny cardboard: it won't help. 'The only trick anyone's ever used to make their business plan stand out that worked was when they sent it in with a bottle of champagne,' remembers one VC. 'Although I have to say I didn't end up investing in their company.'

The structure of a business plan

Executive summary

This is usually a condensed, concise and convincing two or three page document that summarises the whole of the business plan. Typically, this is what you will initially send out to VCs and other investors. If they like what they read they will then contact you to be sent the full plan. Clearly then, the executive summary has to do a spectacular sales job, but it mustn't be a piece of PR puff or contain an obvious sales pitch. It is the hardest part to write, but if you get it right it will make writing the rest of the plan much easier.

'In the first paragraph I want to see two things,' says Tim Hammond of Ideas Hub. 'I want to know what the business is and why the management team want to do it.' The motivation of the management team is not quite so important in conventional business plans, but in the current internet climate, the management team's unique claims to be the best placed, best motivated and best connected people to drive an idea to an initial public offering (IPO) is a powerful piece of information to include.

In a series of well written paragraphs, the executive summary should give the reader:

1. A synopsis of the company – its strategy and its unique selling proposition (USP).

2. A brief description of the market (it's likely that an investor will have no knowledge of your market) and the competition.

3. A quick description of your site and its purpose.

4. Quick biographies of the management team and their unique qualities that guarantee the business the greatest chance of success.

5. A forecast of the financial potential of the company.

6. The amount of money you are looking to raise and the amount an investor is likely to make.

7. The likely exit strategy for the investor (for example, an IPO on the stock exchange or a trade sale).

In short, for an executive summary to convince an investor to read the rest of your business plan, it must contain the energy you feel for your site, it must put your idea into the context of the market and must convince him or her that yours is the best approach to capture the hearts and wallets of that market. Crucially, it has to contain a clear indication of the likely return the investor will make on his investment.

A description and history of the company

This section of the business plan should convey the

company vision. For example, it shouldn't just be that you want to create an online learning centre for the unemployed. It should be that you want to empower the disenfranchised and take a stake in your users' futures. It should stop short of 'I want to rule the world' but it should be exciting as well as convincing.

You then have to show how the company will reach its potential. This is your Business Concept which should describe your company's structure and purpose and should make reference to similar companies (ideally in America) to give an idea of your potential for growth. It should outline your unique elements and succinctly convey your company in a few paragraphs. The next area you need to cover is your Profit Model. This basically means telling the investor how you intend to make your money, be it through advertising, e-commerce, subscription or offline activities, or a combination of these revenue streams. It's legitimate with e-businesses to make a reference to your potential worth based on your profits and the value of your users. Investors like to put a ballpark value on your company (this allows them to assess how much equity their investment is equal to) and this is usually done by taking your forecasted earnings at the end of a certain period (generally three or five years' time) and multiplying them by a factor specific to your industry. The factor for most businesses is usually between five and ten: for internet companies it was at one time as high as 40 as the anticipated rates of growth for e-businesses were so spectacular. Stock market fluctuations have deflated such valuations.

For example, if at the end of three years your company is predicted to produce profits of £10 million, this figure is multiplied by anything up to 40 to produce a figure of anything up to £400 million. This is the value it is assumed the company would reach if it was sold or floated on the stock exchange. Now you can see how internet companies that are only a few months old and operating at a loss come up with these vastly inflated valuations. An investor will be well aware of this trick, but it can be worthwhile including a calculation to demonstrate the size of your vision.

Before you get carried away with being a millionaire, you will also need to describe in this section your history to date, which might be working in the front room on a borrowed computer – or even less if you're trying to raise funds at the concept stage. Simply state the achievements of the company so far, mentioning when you launched, how the launch was funded, any advertising or marketing deals already in place etc.

You now need to convey your immediate and long term plans for the company and how you to intend to manage its growth. It's a good idea to use graphs and illustrations wherever possible as it conveys at a glance what could otherwise take paragraphs.

If you have any advisors or partners you should mention them here. They don't have to be traditional business advisors, but an Advisory Board with relevant business experience that you can call on for advice or introductions goes a long way to convince an investor that you have the support and influence you need to succeed.

This is also the point at which you could include press cuttings about your company or your industry or testimonials from users – this helps an investor to visualise the impact and importance of your company in its market.

At this point you should tell an investor about the legal structure of your company. Are you a limited company or a partnership? Who owns the company? Is it owned equally by the management team or are there additional people with a stake in the company (perhaps an initial investor or professional advisor)?

An analyis of the market and the competition

Be prepared for the research you need to do to write this part of the business plan properly to change the direction of your company! If you researched this area thoroughly when you were still at the idea stage it shouldn't pose too many problems, but even if you did, do the research again. In the months since you last checked the competition several rivals could have launched. This is the internet, and money can move fast and with stealth – you need to be constantly aware of the changing mood of the market.

Don't assume that your investor will know about your market, but you stand a greater chance of getting funding if you target an investor with an interest in your market so the information you give here must be accurate and objective.

The information you need to give here is:

✦ the size of the current market (plus the potential size for the market allowing for future take-up of the internet);

✦ an analysis of the consumers who make up that market;

✦ a reasonably detailed report on other websites that are in the market (or in current net jargon 'occupy the same space' as your site);

✦ a realistic projection of your company's future market share based on demonstrable predictions; and

✦ any legal concerns or regulations that affect your industry (this might include references to competition rules or patent and copyright information).

Revenue streams

If a VC is really interested in your concept, the information you provide here will be vital in convincing him or her to take things to the next stage. You need to clearly define who your customers are and how you can make money out of them: you should demonstrate how you fulfil your users' needs. Describe each sort of customer you have – you might have some who buy products from you as well as some who visit your site just to get information. Both sorts of customers are important as advertisers will be interested in reaching both.

You need to give some sort of profile of your users, whether they're foreign exchange dealers accessing your financial data site or new parents seeking nappy changing advice. You need to make it obvious why people will visit, and revisit, your site. You then need to provide details about the average earnings of your customers, their online use and the advertisers who currently spend millions trying to reach your market.

Taking each of your revenue streams (advertising, e-commerce, subscription etc.) in turn, describe how you will access your users for profit.

Marketing plan

A creative and cost-effective marketing plan is a key success differentiator in internet companies, and investors will want to know how you intend to advertise your site to users. If you want to launch a business-to-consumer site (B2C) the current thinking is that you will spend some-where between 70 and 90 per cent of your budget on marketing just to get your URL, message and brand heard above the background noise of endless dotcoms vying for consumers' attention. You should list here PR and advertising agencies you plan to work with (these should be companies you have a genuine agreement to work with after you have secured funding) and how you will target your users. Will it be an online campaign, will you sponsor *Coronation Street* or will you simply hand out leaflets in the street and shout at shoppers through a megaphone? Give as much detail as possible.

Operating plan

This section of your business plan should ideally contain three elements: the structure of the company (chain of command etc.), the planned growth of the company (the timings for taking on staff or introducing new services to your site) and the key processes involved in delivering on the predictions made in your vision statement. If you know your business, this shouldn't take very long at all because basically you're just telling an investor how you will put your plan into action. Try to break it down into easy to understand paragraphs (use headings like 'Staffing', 'Growth' and 'Structure') that contain as much detail as possible (such as salaries, union implications, the timings and catalysts for expansion etc.). To demonstrate the company structure some kind of diagram is always useful.

Financial forecasts and data

Every business plan has a spreadsheet attached to it (usually on disk or emailed as an attachment, as this is something investors like to play around with) and a series of graphs and illustrations to show revenues versus costs. The spreadsheet will contain detailed financial information from the cost of your office electricity bill to revenues from affiliate marketing.

While it's impossible to accurately predict the exact costs of running a business, you need to make informed predictions about your likely outgoings and income. By working out your costs and income on a quarter by quarter (or month by month) basis, you can see how much money you need to raise and by when.

Along with this data, you need to provide a sensitivity analysis which, put simply, outlines the margin for error in your calculations. For instance, if your sensitivity analysis reveals that your advertising revenue could slump by half for whatever reason, an investor will want to halve your earnings throughout the spreadsheet to see what that does to future profits. It is by playing around with the figures and the sensitivity analysis that an investor accurately assesses the risks of investing in your company.

Appendices

Sometimes the number of pages in the appendices can outnumber the pages in the body of the business plan. Typically these include profit and loss sheets, a detailed organisational structure (especially if your company will expand internationally and may end up with a complicated ownership structure), additional financial information (usually a series of graphs showing exponential increases in profits!), a short-term implementation plan, the CVs and profiles of the management team and contact details in case investors want to set up a meeting.

Make sure you can agree with all the following statements before sending out your business plan to investors:

My executive summary tells an investor what the company does, why the management team is doing it and how much money they are likely to make over a given time period. ☐

The business plan makes me excited about my company. ☐

Reading my business plan makes it easier for me to visualise the future of my company. ☐

Reading my business plan gives an investor a clear idea about what makes my company unique. ☐

My business plan is based on accurate and reasonable assumptions. ☐

Directory

There are sites that have sample business plans you can look at, sites that help you write your business plan and sites that simply offer advice. Here is a good selection.

http://www.dtonline.com/writing/wrcover.htm
Deloitte and Touche: extensive tips on business plan writing

http://wsj.miniplan.com/
Wall Street Journal Start-up: read some sample business plans relevant to your business

http://www.bplans.com
B Plans: more sample plans

http://www.sba.gov/starting/indexbusplans.html
Totally comprehensive step-by-step guide to writing your business plan from this useful US site

http://www.bcentral.com/directory/bizplan.html
List of links to business plan resources from those helpful people at Microsoft and lots more besides

http://www.morebusiness.com/templates_worksheets/bplans/
Sample business plans and marketing plan

http://www.patentcafe.com/smallbiz_cafe/businessplan.html
Links to programs that help the business plan process

http://www.webcom.com/seaquest/sbrc/busplan.html
Another perspective on that perfect plan

http://www.brs-inc.com/plans.org/mootcorp.html
Dozens of example business plans for you to analyse

http://www.vfinance.com/buspl_down_app.asp
Download a business plan template in Word for free

http://www.bizplanit.com
Compose a business plan online here

Entrepreneur Profile | Graham Goodkind

1. Name

Graham Goodkind

2. Age

34

3. URL of your business

another.com

4. What is the purpose/nature of your business/website?

Free web-based email with a twist – choose from over 10,000 domain names, have whatever you want before the @ sign, and create unique and memorable email addresses. Have up to 20 email addresses all operated from the one account!

5. Date your business started

Originally founded in 1998 by myself, Jeremy Kerner and Steve Bowbrick. Went live to the public in May 1999.

6. Is this your first new media venture?

Yes.

7. Briefly describe your previous business experience and state how useful this was in starting your site.

My previous job was managing director of Lynne Franks PR, the 'alleged' inspiration for the TV show *Absolutely Fabulous*. I spent 10 years there, starting as a trainee account executive and working my way up, learning the ins and outs of marketing communication and working with some of the UK's leading marketing companies, both blue chip and young innovative companies. A few years ago I started up a new media division at the agency (we launched the then little-known company called Excite in the UK), anticipating that the internet would become something with which marketers had to get to grips. I had always been interested in the internet – not from a tech perspective but from a consumer experience – and saw how marketing could play a pivotal role in the market. That experience and insight has been invaluable for another.com.

8. Briefly outline your educational qualifications. Please state which universities/colleges you got these qualifications from.

Three A-levels (A, B, B), one S-level – University College School.
BA(Hons) Business Studies (Marketing) – Guildhall University.

9. Were you able to/did you try to raise seed financing from family and friends? If so, how much did you raise?

One of the founders, Jeremy Kerner, provided £250,000 which was the seed financing.

10. Did you have any useful contacts when it came to raising finance? If so, what kind of introductions proved to be the most useful?

Didn't really need the networking groups which have become quite famous. Personal contacts prevailed!

11. Roughly how much money did you raise in venture capital and was this enough?

As the £250,000 was burning out, we had to decide on the next funding route. At the time, VC money was not as (readily) available as it is now and the terms of doing a deal were much less exciting for the entrepreneur. We decided to raise money – approx £5 million – by floating a stake in the company on the AIM. Our flotation was due at the end of July, prior to Freeserve, when there were only a handful of dotcoms listed in the UK. It was ambitious and proved to be very well received in the City. The prospectus had been written, all the presentations and investor roadshows done and we were three days from the day of impact when we received an offer from a private investment fund – Eden Capital – which we accepted. Our announcement of flotation had given us tremendous exposure – a great form of PR in itself! – and we agreed a deal whereby they bought a straight 20 per cent stake for £6.25 million in cash. It exceeded our expectations from a float and also allowed us the (relative) freedom from the constraints of the City to get on and develop our business. It was a great deal.

12. How many people were there on your management team?

Steve and I ran and still run the company on a day-to-day basis. Jeremy has other interests and devotes a day or so a week equivalent in time. We quicky got an interim COO who has bags of experience in operations management. And then we recruited a team of people and management around us. We now employ about 20 people with a further 10 or so 'full-time' contractors. When we did the Eden deal there was one full-time employee – our systems admin guy!

13. How useful have you found networking events like First Tuesday and BoobNight?

Have never been to either to be honest, although my partner Steve has been to a couple. Because everyone else is doing it is a good reason in my mind not to do it!

14. What would you do differently if you had to start all over again?

Have not really got far enough yet to really say what we'd have done differently. I suppose, with hindsight, we could have moved a lot quicker in our employment. We've been quite selective and discerning in our recruitment as opposed to what I often feel other firms are doing, which appears to be recruiting willy-nilly. Somewhere in between would probably have been better for us.

15. What do you think are the criteria that have most helped you make a success of your business (e.g. having first mover advantage, a brilliant marketing campaign, bloody-mindedness)?

I think it's basically that we're sitting on a bloody great idea. Think about it. Someone telling you who your identity has to be? You having a

.freeserve.net or .tesco.net suffix to your name – excuse me, are they paying you??! What does having .waitrose.com at the end of your identity say about you?? Doesn't having hotmail.com after your name, which you'll never be able to get anyway, imply a certain lack of imagination? We're getting to the stage of the development of the internet now where people will start to examine their online identities more closely.

Your email address is the one definitive way of identifying you in the online arena – people will want to take control of their identity and let it say something about them (rather than being dictated to). The idea is the core. The brand is the business too! And we're only just starting to play with the power of the another.com brand – the name is so superb!

16. What's been the hardest thing you've had to face since starting your business?

Balancing the opinions of the other shareholders and reaching consensus. Personally, I've always been quite single-minded and focused. Having to debate and discuss things with others and having differences of opinions are frustrating and need resolution. I dislike all the talk and love the action.

17. What's the most useful piece of advice you've been given?

If you can't convince them, confuse them.

18. What's the one piece of advice you wish someone had given you, but didn't?

Take out insurance on having twins – my wife's just given birth to Dexter and Summer!

19. Do you believe it's still possible for someone with only a good idea and determination to succeed in new media – or is it all about raising money these days?

Someone with a good idea and determination will usually succeed, not just in new media. Plenty of people can have (and do have) a good idea – it's only the ones who carry them out who succeed. Money is no substitute for that. Having said that, raising money is a lot about who you know these days as well and that can also be important.

20. Are you in profit?

No.

6 | Raising finance

ALTHOUGH IT'S PERFECTLY POSSIBLE TO start an internet company and get a website built and marketed for next to no money, in the current climate it is virtually impossible to grow a business organically. Every Internet business that intends to make serious money needs a massive injection of cash to compete, and ultimately to succeed.

There are several sources you can go to for finance, ranging from family and friends to global investment funds.

Every internet business that intends to make serious money needs a massive injection of cash to compete, and ultimately to succeed.

You can find people who will just give you money, or you can find funding from companies that will also give you guidance and strategic and operational support. All these sources of funding will be explained shortly, but first it's important to get a bit of background on how internet investment currently works.

A few years ago, getting funding for an internet

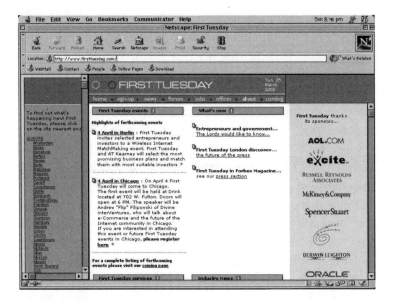

company was nigh on impossible. Tim Hammond, who launched the shopping portal myTaxi (*www.mytaxi.com*) in 1996, remembers: 'We had to educate not just the public that they could shop online but we also had to persuade investors that there was money in e-commerce!' It seems incredible now. Even in the middle of 1999 there were stories of investors writing out cheques for a quarter of a million for seed financing for start-ups at First Tuesday events. While fundraising is still frenetic it is less frenzied these days with more and more ideas languishing without funding.

Virtually every day there is a story in the business pages of national newspapers about a company setting up an internet investment arm, such is the paranoia among big businesses that they might be missing out on the next big wave. But for every fund that's set up there are hundreds of people sitting at home thinking up ideas for internet businesses. 'I don't think there's a shortage of ideas,' says Hammond, who is now the CEO of the incubator Ideas Hub, 'but there is definitely a shortage of good management teams to implement those ideas.'

Fund managers and investors aren't stupid: if they were they wouldn't be rich. They generally have specific criteria they need to have met before handing over the dosh. Getting funding for your website may take a long time and you might have to send your business plan to hundreds of people before you get even a sniff of money out of them. And if your idea is still just that, then you are going to have to work even harder to prove your commitment and ability to investors. Before you start approaching investors, you need to think long and hard about the sort of money you want. Do you want the hands-on support of an incubator or an investor that leaves you alone until they receive your annual report? This chapter will help you decide on the best people to approach for your particular plan. Dr Matthias Calice of Apax Partners, one of the big venture capitalist firms, has this advice:

'If your idea is to build a nice little niche business it might not

be a good idea to approach a large fund whose business it is to grow billion dollar companies. First of all you need to target the right fund, then you need to get some sort of attention through networking to find someone who can recommend you to that fund.'

Looking out for sharks

If you're completely new to big business and million dollar budgets, there's no point in pretending to be a big cheese when you're really just a Baby Bel. Equally, never let on just how green you are: you must be smart as you will come across a lot of people who want to take a piece of your company away from you. It's quite common for agencies and individuals to say they will work for you or make introductions on your behalf for some equity in your firm. Equity is common currency in internet-land and while it might be the only way of paying a bill for a new company with no earnings, you need to be very careful about frittering away your equity.

If you're completely new to big business and million dollar budgets, there's no point in pretending to be a big cheese when you're really just a Baby Bel.

One female entrepreneur remembers: 'When my partner – who is also female – and I first started to build a network of contacts with the aim of getting investment we had a lot of men saying "I'll get you some funding, love, just give me 20 per cent of your company". I don't know whether we got the blonde treatment just because we were female, but there did seem to be a lot of sharks preying on inexperienced entrepreneurs when we got started.'

When you don't know very much about raising finance, or business at all for that matter, it can be very tempting to

No one will ever work as hard at raising finance – or doing anything for your company – as you will.

take someone up on their offer to 'take care of you'. Be very wary of people making such offers: not only are they probably chancers who are just hoping that one of the companies they have a stake in will take off, but if you think someone who says they know what they're doing is taking care of the finance there is a temptation to relax. No one will ever work as hard at raising finance – or doing anything for your company – as you will. And the more you rely on third parties to do the hard work for you, the less you will learn and the less likely it will be that you will develop the skills you will need to turn your idea into a success.

If you do feel you need help raising the funds, look to your financial adviser, solicitor or accountant for help, or keep on networking until you find someone who will help you for just a small amount of equity, perhaps around the five per cent mark.

'One of the biggest mistakes we see start-ups making,' says Amory Hall of strategic web agency methodfive, 'is giving away too much equity. Typically companies will have to give away equity for a seed round of financing, a first and second round and then have to give still more away to employees. People who have given away too much too soon simply can't manoeuvre properly in the future.'

How an internet company raises finance

The typical way an internet company raises finance is like this:

Stage 1

Raise £50,000 to £500,000 in a seed round of financing from private sources or incubator funds. For this expect to give away between 10 and 40 per cent of your company. At this point you get to tell everyone your company is worth £X million meaning that you, if your stake in the company is large enough, are a paper millionaire!

Stage 2

Raise your second round of finance, usually between £1 million and £20 million, either from an investment fund or a strategic partner. As the company is more valuable now than it was when you gave up equity for the first round, you should be giving away five to 15 per cent (possibly up to 40 per cent for large sums) at this stage.

Stage 3

Not every company gets to this stage, but some net firms need a massive injection of cash (possibly over £100 million) to do things like set up branches in 20 cities worldwide virtually overnight. Often this money is raised on the stock market, but it's not uncommon for it to come from a consortium of partners prior to an IPO (initial public offering, or flotation). These types of deal are generally top secret and no one will ever tell you how much equity was on the negotiating table. Many companies are continually raising funds – fourth and fifth rounds are not unheard of.

The best way to approach anyone for investment is via someone who can recommend you. If you know any other entrepreneurs who have received funding, then get them to make introductions to a fund manager on your behalf. Or maybe you know an accountant or a solicitor or financial adviser that has some access to investors. Ask around.

Failing that, you should try to meet an investor at a networking event. Fewer and fewer investors turn up to the networking events run by First Tuesday and the mainstream matchmaking meetings, but there are other events organised by Surf's Up (*www.surfsup.org.uk*), BOOBnight (*www.boobnight.co.uk*) and We Gather (a female network run by *www.esouk.com*) and there are new ones springing up regularly around the country. There are fewer opportunities outside London even though First Tuesday now has regular events in Edinburgh, Glasgow and regional cities in England; however, your local Chamber of Commerce or Enterprise Agency may organise something. Try to register for entry to an event (you can often do this via their sites) and attend with your pockets stuffed full of business cards. You might not meet an investor, but you might meet someone who knows one!

If you can't get access to an investor then you need to send your executive summary to them by post or email. But do your research first. Use the information in this chapter and the links in the directory to work out exactly the sorts of projects investors are looking for. Almost all of them have websites that will tell you how much money they typically invest, at what stage they invest in a company (many of the larger firms don't consider giving seed finance), and what industries they are interested in investing in. The websites will also usually tell you how they like to receive business plans. Some websites actually allow you to apply online.

ESouk.com, a company that calls itself an internet accelerator, allows entrepreneurs to make their pitch online and one of its directors, Graham Hodge, says entrepreneurs shouldn't be worried about giving out their ideas in such a fashion.

'It's a very good way for people to approach us. If they fill in the form on the website it's guaranteed that it will get looked at

within a couple of days. If they leave a message, it might not get returned, and emails get lost. It's actually a very effective way for entrepreneurs to get noticed. In the past entrepreneurs never sent out a business plan or even an executive summary without getting an NDA signed, but that's changed.'

An NDA (a Non Disclosure Agreement) or confidentiality notice is a legal document that investors sometimes sign before reading business plans. These prevent them from telling a third party about your idea. In practice, few investors will sign an NDA these days – and that's not because they plan to rip you off.

'We get sent 100 business plans a week. If we were to sign NDAs for each of those we would need a legal department bigger than the rest of the company to cope.'

In practice, there has only been one case so far in which a company successfully sought compensation from an investor who had given details to someone else. One case of plagiarism out of hundreds of thousands of business plans sent out: there's not a great reason to worry as most of the time it's more bother than it's worth trying to pilfer someone else's idea. The other reason VCs and investors are reluctant to sign NDAs is because they will often see several plans with the same idea. 'Whatever brilliant idea you've had you can bet at least 20 other people have also had it,' says Tim Hammond.

> *Whatever brilliant idea you've had you can bet at least 20 other people have also had it.*

Venture capitalists and incubators are usually investing in management teams, not ideas, so it doesn't pay to be overly protective of your idea. Forcing a VC to sign an NDA is a good way to make sure you won't get investment. If you are worried about the theft of your idea, assemble a shit-hot management team before telling anyone else about it. The best management team is the best protection you can get for your idea.

Once an investor has read your executive summary and likes it, the next stage is to either request to see the full business plan or to arrange a meeting. If you get to this stage you have good reason to feel confident as typically less than 10 per cent of management teams get this far. The bad news is that you are probably still two or three meetings away from getting the cash.

Good money versus bad money

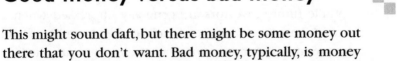

This might sound daft, but there might be some money out there that you don't want. Bad money, typically, is money that you give away too much equity for or that comes with strings attached. Sometimes these strings might just be that the deal is heavily weighted in the investor's favour (this might be something like a non-dilution agreement that means the investor's share isn't reduced by further rounds of finance) but not necessarily too onerous. Sometimes though, bad money comes with certain terms and conditions that prevent you running your company the way you want.

Sometimes investors insist on a seat on the board. This is often just a way for them to give guidance and to ensure their money is being spent wisely. Sometimes though, investors can start throwing their weight around and vetoing your plans or insisting you use certain suppliers etc. Before you take someone's money be very sure about how they see a long-term relationship evolving. Equally, bad money can be from an indifferent investor who just lets you run your own show when you really need advice. The key thing for an entrepreneur to do is to identify what they want from an investor. If you need extra help, then an incubator might provide you with 'good' money. Conversely, if you need millions, giving away 30 per cent in equity for £250,000 at the seed stage is 'bad' money because you are running out of equity to hand over for the millions you'll need to succeed.

While future investors are generally impressed when a start-up has raised any cash at all, be mindful of the reputation of your investor: will their name attached to your project give you credibility problems?

Bad money can sometimes become good money if the timing's right, and vice versa. 'When we were setting up myTaxi we spent too much time raising the money,' remembers Tim Hammond. 'Looking back we might have been better off taking a slightly worse deal where the timing had been better.' When your back's up against the wall an investor is in a strong position and can place all sorts of conditions on the deal. Generally this is bad money, but it's better than going under.

'One of the biggest mistakes I see entrepreneurs making is taking the wrong money,' says Apax's Calice.

What are investors looking for?

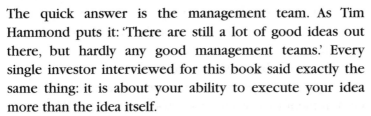

The quick answer is the management team. As Tim Hammond puts it: 'There are still a lot of good ideas out there, but hardly any good management teams.' Every single investor interviewed for this book said exactly the same thing: it is about your ability to execute your idea more than the idea itself.

That doesn't mean that your management team has to be made up of four people, one with an MBA, another a technical genius, another with specialist knowledge of your target industry and a marketing wunderkind who will make the whole world remember your name. A management team can be made up of one individual if you're just looking for seed financing (some incubators and business angels will help you put together a management team if you can convince them of your commitment and ability to execute your idea). 'A good management team is one where the skills fit the opportunity,' says Matthias Calice. 'We look for a complementary team that has some experience of what they're trying to do. Serial entrepreneurs are ideal as they know what it takes to get a company off the ground.' Big management teams aren't always better either: 'Sometimes you can have too many people on the same level and this can lead to instability,' says one investor.

If your management team is a bit weak, then approaching an incubator is a smart move. As eSouk's Graham Hodge says: 'We're not necessarily looking for well rounded management teams as we have many of the necessary skills in-house. It's appealing to get someone with very relevant experience of the sector their site will operate in.'

While your business acumen may single you out for funding, some people are more interested in your commitment to a certain plan. 'You can see it in their eyes,' says Hammond. 'There is the difference between someone who walks in and opens up their laptop to give you a PowerPoint demonstration and those who walk in and evangelise about their idea. Usually that's far more compelling.' Calice agrees: 'We look for people who are driven by the idea. People who don't take no for an answer, who don't stop building the business to raise the finance but for whom the money is a by-product.' Many firms are impressed if you can show that you have built a site and fledgling business from scratch before seeking funding, but others know how hard it is to run a business effectively without backing – or while you're looking for backing.

Investors will also be looking for ideas that match their investment criteria. If you only want £100,000 there's not much point approaching a company like Atlas Venture that rarely invests less than £5 million. 'The most compelling thing for Ideas Hub is when we can put a lot of value into a project,' says Tim Hammond. 'That's usually early stage and we like to see that we can bring it to market quicker than anyone else.'

Obviously, the other key ingredient investors will want to see is a Bloody Good Idea. It doesn't necessarily have to be an original one, although that helps. 'A "me too" idea can't make it now,' says one incubator manager. 'Equally, sometimes an idea is so left field that it will take too much time and effort to bring it to market. They're often the projects you'd like to get involved with but can't because they will prevent you from spending time with other management teams.'

For some investors, a variation on a 'me too' idea is appealing. As discussed in previous chapters, having an idea to sell books online isn't going to get funding any more, but finding a canny twist or loophole in someone else's idea can prove financially rewarding. 'First mover advantage isn't as important as it once was,' explains one VC. 'Having a clear market advantage is much more important.' Finally, the one detail every investor will look closely at is the money you will make for them. Make sure you can offer them a tenfold return on their investment.

Types of investor

Banks

Even last year, banks were very reluctant to lend to internet ventures as the risk was seen as too high. Since the hype really took off, more and more banks are lending to internet entrepreneurs as they are scared of missing out on their slice of the pie. As a general rule, high street banks are a bad source of income for internet entrepreneurs as they have little experience and can provide little guidance. They also make you pay money back instead of taking equity stakes (although this is not unheard of) and the repayments can badly affect the short term profitability of your company. Typically, banks tend to loan small amounts and this is rarely enough for internet ventures in the current climate.

Often any loan will be secured against the assets of the management team, usually their homes. If you can't make the repayments you run the risk of repossession (although, as you can imagine, this is one hell of a motivation to make sure your company succeeds).

This doesn't mean that you don't want to make friends with your bank. Many of the high street banks offer free banking to new businesses, and they can also provide business advice and support. Keeping your bank's business advisor informed of your company's progress might come in handy if you ever need a temporary loan to cover a shortfall. Be mindful not to use up all your credit at once – you never know when you might need to go cap in hand to your bank.

Friends and family

Rich parents or a friend who's just had a big redundancy package could be very useful people to have to hand as you plan your business. Most of us, though, know very few people with enough money to make ends meet, let alone invest thousands in an untried venture. If you can rustle up a rich aunt though, this is definitely the time to do it!

Rich parents or a friend who's just had a big redundancy package could be very useful people to have to hand as you plan your business.
If you can rustle up a rich aunt though, this is definitely the time to do it!

Getting backing from people you know has several advantages (we'll come to the disadvantages later). First, it's quick. One pint down the pub or a brilliantly prepared Sunday roast and the cheque's in the post. No endless rounds of negotiation, or poring over spreadsheets. Second, people who are playing with loved ones' money tend to be incredibly motivated to avoid failure. Third, having any kind of investment attracts more money: investors are like sheep.

The downside to money from family and friends needs to be seriously considered though. Sometimes it can be an unnecessary added stress (for this reason NEVER allow someone to invest their nest egg or pension) as you feel a

Having any kind of investment attracts more money: investors are like sheep.

tremendous obligation to succeed. Also you might have your old dad breathing down your neck telling you how he did things in his day. Letting a relative or friend feel some sense of ownership over your company is definitely a BAD idea. Loyalty often means that you end up giving away more equity than you would to an anonymous funder. The other drawback to this kind of funding is that it often comes without expertise.

There is one source of income that might be worth seeking from your immediate circle - your boss. Your boss may choose to invest in your idea - especially if it's to do with the industry he or she already operates in - for two reasons: one is that they don't want to lose such a motivated, intelligent and ambitious employee, the other (and this is far more likely) is that they won't want to see you trot off to anyone else for funding.

Business angels

The concept of the business angel is much better developed in America where a 'high risk, high reward' culture has been in existence for decades. A business angel is usually a businessman (yup, they are mostly men) who has made a personal fortune as an entrepreneur himself. Having sold his company he now entertains himself by investing smallish amounts (usually £50,000 to £250,000) in new companies and giving younger entrepreneurs the benefit of his experience.

Business angels get very involved in the companies they invest in, often assuming a chairman role to the entrepreneur's chief executive. In the directory at the end of this chapter you will find a website listing most British business angels to help you find one with experience of your sector. A good angel will be a motivating force that can provide contacts and cash, but a bad angel will take over and treat you like a child. In many instances the sort of advice a business angel can provide should be the sort of information you can get from your advisory board, but the added hands-on business acumen can be a godsend. However, one entrepreneur who insisted on anonymity said the following:

A good angel will be a motivating force that can provide contacts and cash, but a bad angel will take over and treat you like a child

'Being based outside of London where all the big funds have their offices, we were keen to find local finance. We thought we had done very well when a prominent local businessman who was a councillor invested in us. He was excellent at providing us with contacts and making introductions and his money came in useful too. But – and this sounds awful – he was nearly 60 and didn't really understand the full implications of the internet. Sometimes we would overhear him talking to people about us and just cringe because he sounded so naff spouting jargon he didn't understand.'

Increasingly, however, with internet entrepreneurs taking their businesses to the stock exchange before their thirtieth birthdays, there will be more and more internet millionaires with relevant business experience out there looking for new companies to get involved with.

Strategic partners

One of the smartest fundraising strategies is to get money from companies already operating in your 'space'. For example, one entrepreneur set up a site for the circus and funfair industry and raised £2 million in funding from everyone from big theme parks to travelling circuses in Europe and America. Not only does he now have access to the best spread of expertise and contacts in his target industry, but he can negotiate supply deals on the best terms. In addition – and this is the really smart bit – all of his potential rivals have been turned into partners who have no interest in investing in a competing site.

Strategic partners can often bring industry expertise, clout and contacts to the table, and for small sites the clout is the most valuable of those. Aligning yourself with a bigger, better-known company can help others take you more seriously and can open doors other sorts of investment can't. If it's important for your site to be independent editorially then this might not be the right move for you, but having an industry giant behind you is a great security when times get tough.

There are risks associated with this kind of investment though. If you take your fabulous idea for a webcasting site to a broadcaster, they might be better placed to launch such a site themselves. In this situation, you must insist on getting an NDA signed (most investment companies will let you have a copy of a standard NDA – sometimes they are available on their websites – that you can alter to fit your requirements).

The best way to approach strategic partners is through personal contacts. If you don't have any, phone up and ask to speak to the head of new business development and sound out the possibility of them investing in an outside project: be cagey – you do not want to give away any unnecessary information.

Incubators

'Incubators exist because there is a shortfall between the money venture capitalists look to invest and the sums needed by start-up firms. There are a lot of fantastic projects that previously couldn't attract funding attention because they required relatively small amounts of cash and were below the radar screens of the big funds.'

Tim Hammond

As their name suggests, with an incubator you get a fair bit of nurturing as part of the package. Graham Hodge of eSouk.com says: 'In addition to money we also give hands-on advice, strategic advice, admin support and space in our office.' Essentially the incubator package takes a lot of the day-to-day hassles out of the early stages of starting a company: you don't have to worry about finding offices, finding accountants or waste time trying to work out PAYE. You can then dedicate more of your time to your business strategy and getting your site up and running.

Typically, incubators get involved in companies at very early stages, sometimes when there's little more than an idea, an ambition and a five or six page business plan. They usually invest between £50,000 and £500,000 and take a 10 to 40 per cent stake in a company. They usually work with companies for between four months and two years and help them raise the next round of finance.

For green entrepreneurs with little experience, incubators can seem an attractive and safe option. Even for more ambitious and experienced entrepreneurs, they still provide a smooth entry into the dizzy world of corporate finance. Alfie Nwawudu's company hobomedia.com has been incubated by Brainspark (*www.brainspark.com*) since the end of 1999. 'It's been a very good move for us,' he explains. 'Working in this office has really allowed us to develop a network of contacts that would have been impossible otherwise. Whatever problems we have there is someone here who faced the same situation a few months ago and can help us out.' The Brainspark office, like many incubators, has a feverish atmosphere where 20 or so companies share facilities. Just about the only things the companies have in common is their age (they're all under a year old) and the fact that they have an internet application. 'Given how diverse these companies are, it's fascinating to see that many of us have had the same problems.'

Aside from problem solving and support, incubators can be good for other reasons. 'I suppose there's a bit of competition between us, and that's a good motivator,' says another of Brainspark's inmates. 'it's not just the motivation you get with an incubator; as a young company it gives us credibility with clients and investors.' Another benefit is that incubators can help you keep your operating costs down in the first few months of trading. 'We don't have to hire consultants or outside help,' says Nwawudu, 'because someone somewhere in this room has got all the answers.'

Unsurprisingly, those involved with incubators are evangelical in their comments about these business accelerators. 'I was speaking to a colleague in America,' says Hammond, 'who told me that the latest figures from VCs were that they only expected one in 10 of the companies they were investing in to still be going two years after funding. I think the figure for incubated companies is around 85 per cent still in business. We would certainly expect that four out of every five companies we worked with to be still viable after two years and that the rest wouldn't just fold, but would merge or change their business model in some way.' Strategic partners are often attracted to invest in incubated companies, although VCs have differing opinions about putting money into incubator protégés. 'It seems logical to me that an investor would be more interested in a company that's been through our process,' says eSouk's Hodge. However, few incubated companies turn into FTSE 100 companies. 'There is a feeling,' says one VC, 'that a management team that chooses to go to an incubator doesn't have the drive, commitment or ability to go it alone. Management teams without conviction and contacts can't produce the kind of return we are looking for.'

If you are looking into getting involved with an incubator, be careful about (a) giving away too much equity for a relatively small amount of money and (b) giving up too much control. 'We found that we let the managers of the incubator make decisions for our company that probably weren't right,' reveals a first time entrepreneur. 'But we felt that they knew what they were doing and we didn't feel qualified enough to contradict them.'

Different incubators work in different ways. Some will be very hands-on for four or five months and work closely with you, raising enough finance for you so that you can fly the nest relatively quickly. Others work on a safety net model and will let you use their services and offices for up to two years before expecting you to fly solo.

Venture Capitalists

This is the area of fundraising that seems to be the most difficult to enter for bedroom or first-time entrepreneurs. And yet it is the actions of the VCs in the past year that has encouraged so many people to have a go at launching an e-business. The millions and millions of pounds flowing into dotcoms has made a lot of people think that there are VCs who will give money to anything that moves. The common perception is that VCs behave like racing fans betting on every horse in the race: if they invest in enough companies one of them will make enough money to recoup the funds distributed to all the rest. Every VC interviewed for this book said that this kind of 'portfolio' investing wasn't something their company did, but in practice it's clear that a lot of money is being invested unwisely. 'The problem is that we've all been caught up in the hype,' explains one European fund manager, 'and last year's budget for investment has been tripled this year. We are being given so much more money to put into dotcoms and it is our job to spend it.' The general acceptance seems to be that investors are getting so many applications for finance that they are not making enough checks on entrepreneurs' plans. Therefore it follows that in the current climate, projects that would normally be shown the door are being shown the money.

'I think what is really happening is that VCs are looking at people's plans and looking for ways to maximise their stakes in these new companies,' says one industry observer. 'I worked with an entrepreneur who took his plan to a fund manager asking for £5 million and he was offered £15 million. The investor said it would allow him to grow his company more quickly and prevent the need for a further round of financing. He also took 60 per cent instead of 30 per cent of the company.'

Stories like this aren't uncommon, and while being offered an extra £10 million is a problem many of us would gladly face, there are problems with being diverted from your carefully researched agenda and handing over a larger share of equity than necessary.

Another common story is of an entrepreneur looking for £1 million in venture capital being told – by everyone they meet – to go and rewrite their business plan to make it look like they need £5 million. 'No VC is interested in investing £1 million because they'll never make enough money on that size of investment,' is an oft-repeated mantra in the fundraising world and, by and large, it's true. Venture capitalists are interested in taking stakes in companies with the potential to be global market leaders.

Rob Zegelaar of Atlas Venture says: 'We look to invest between £5 million and £20 million in companies with track records and experienced management teams. We want to grow billion dollar businesses.'

The world of large numbers is not one you can easily penetrate and just about the only way to be taken seriously by a VC is through a recommendation. 'We get about 100 business plans a week sent to us so it's extremely important to see some sort of differentiation in a plan, and usually that's a reference,' explains Matthias Calice of Apax Partners, one of the bigger investment companies.

There are firms that specialise in representing companies to VCs, such as Kick-Start Ventures (*www. kickstartventures.com*), who take small equity stakes in companies in exchange for advice preparing and distributing business plans. A good place to find these intermediaries is through events such as First Tuesday where financial advisers often hang out looking to get involved with entrepreneurs. Many financial advisers have good relationships with fund managers and they can often provide many of the services of an incubator for a much smaller equity stake. Other good people to get to introduce you to VCs are other entrepreneurs, employers, management consultants and bankers.

The next best way to get a venture capitalist's attention is by giving a clear indication of the sort of money you will make for them. They want to see companies through to stock market flotation, companies that will see tremendous growth. They are interested in companies that have developed new ways of finding revenue that could be leveraged in several markets at once.

'Ninety per cent of the time we invest in management teams and not ideas,' says Calice, 'but they need to have a good proposal.' Rob Zegelaar of Atlas Venture says it's vital to have the right balance of knowledge. 'We look to see if management teams have the right mix of domain experience – detailed knowledge of their chosen field – and e-commerce aggressiveness. We see a majority of naive entrepreneurs at the moment, but that is changing as staff leave start-ups to set up on their own.'

Before you approach a VC, do your homework. Check out their site and find out how much money they invest and in what sort of companies. Don't waste your time and theirs by sending them a plan that does not contain their investment criteria.

What happens when you meet an investor

Once an investor – of any persuasion – has seen your business plan and likes it, you will have to meet them. These meetings are usually fairly formal and consist of the entrepreneur making some kind of presentation followed by a question and answer session. As should be abundantly clear by now, the impressiveness of the management team will be the key factor in any investor's decision.

The usual scenario involves making a presentation in PowerPoint or a similar software package outlining the key differentiators in your plan, followed by a tour of your site (if you have one). It's quite hard to make any kind of PowerPoint demonstration memorable and in truth most investors will be watching you rather than your laptop. 'I think we are definitely looking for a degree of showmanship,' says Matthias Calice. 'The CEO's job is to sell the company and they must demonstrate to us that they can do this. Often we get a PowerPoint demonstration but it's not essential: we want a precise and concise picture of the company to be presented and sometimes the way to do this is just to talk.'

Other investors say similar things: they are looking for conviction, energy and absolute knowledge of your market and your unique proposition. They will be looking closely at your team's skills and will want you to demonstrate that you can work together. You should expect your business plan – and every assumption and prediction in it – to be challenged and picked apart. You will be asked about your competition, your long-term goals and your weaknesses.

'Another important factor is that we have to like them,' says Tim Hammond. 'It might sound pretty basic, but if we are going to be working with people hand in glove for several months it's very important to feel that we're going to be able to get on.'

Investors will be trying to ascertain your level of commitment and enthusiasm. As Graham Hodge says: 'It can be very dispiriting seeing people who are just trying to make a fast buck. The compelling ideas are those that have come about because people have experienced problems and hurdles in their fields and they know how their product or service will benefit their users.'

At Ideas Hub, entrepreneurs are given a questionnaire

and the first question is 'Why do you want to do this?'. 'I want to know why someone is motivated to embark on their project,' says Hammond. 'Their motivation is a crucial deciding factor.'

At your first meeting with an investor it is also important that you ask them questions too. You should find out why they're interested in your idea, how you would fit into their portfolio and what kind of advice they can give: you shouldn't seem too grateful for their time.

If you have impressed an investor they will probably go away and conduct their own research into your market and satisfy their own criteria to decide if there is a need for your site. They will probably take up references on the whole of the management team. If that goes well you will almost certainly have to make another presentation, possibly giving much more detail, to more people involved in making the finance decisions.

At this point you will probably be made an offer; i.e. 'we will give you £2 million in exchange for 50 per cent of your company'. Nice as it would be to have the money and desperate as you are by this stage to get it, you must negotiate the best deal possible for your company. 'This is an important negotiation,' says Calice. 'We expect people to be commercial and negotiate hard. If you can't negotiate these terms how will you negotiate terms with suppliers and distributors? We expect people to play hard and fair but always with the view that when the deal is done you no longer sit on opposite sides of the table.'

If your idea and your management team are strong, you may find yourself at the centre of a bidding war where two or more investors want to back you. This is, of course, an ideal situation as you can then get them to bid against each other, reducing the amount of equity you will have to give to them in exchange for funds.

Once you have got to the stage where you have accepted £x for y per cent of your company, it still isn't over. A process called Due Diligence will now take place which basically means your investor's lawyers and accountants will examine your books. They will check that the details you have given them are accurate and that there are no outstanding legal matters which could threaten the company. This process can take weeks or even months (solicitors and accountants have got rich by charging by the hour).

You will need a solicitor yourself at this stage to deal with the redistribution of shares in your company and, if necessary, negotiate some of the finer points of the deal on your behalf (thus preventing you seeming picky or obstructive when dealing with your investor).

After all this, you will finally get your hands on the money and can start devoting yourself to running your business . . . until you need to get the next round of finance in.

Raising finance on the Alternative Investment Market (AIM)

The Alternative Investment Market, operated by the London Stock Exchange, is an increasingly popular way for internet companies to raise finance. It has been developed specifically with young and growing companies in mind. The main requirement is that your company is 'appropriate' for the market. The judgement on your 'appropriateness' is not made by you, however, but by a nominated adviser who must be from a firm of experienced corporate finance professionals approved by the Exchange.

AIM works in pretty much the same way as the London Stock Exchange but trades shares in a much broader range of companies – including those that haven't actually started trading yet. Raising money through AIM isn't right for every company and those that do are subject to stringent regulatory demands. Each company applying to AIM must:

+ appoint a nominated adviser;

+ appoint a nominated broker – this may be the same firm as the nominated adviser;

+ be registered as a plc or equivalent;

+ prepare a prospectus with information on your company and its activities. This includes financial information and any projections, as well as details of all the directors; and

+ pay a flat rate annual fee to the Exchange.

The decision to float on a public market requires much consideration in conjunction with professional advisers who can help you better understand the issues and the choices available to you. These advisers must be brokers, lawyers, accountants or other financial professionals. Funnily enough, none of their services come cheap so you will already need to have several thousand pounds available to enlist their services. You will also need to comply with other rules of the Exchange and these include things like regularly publishing accounts and agreeing that the directors of your company won't trade their own shares for a given period of time.

You will also need to prepare a prospectus for your company informing potential investors about the directors' track records and giving a full description of the company's operations. While the preparation can be time-consuming, the final act of fundraising can be blissfully quick (72 hours after registering with AIM, trading can begin) and this is an option for companies who need to raise funds swiftly. The London Stock Exchange's website has detailed information about joining AIM and has several pdf brochures you can download and peruse at length to help you make a decision. There are also lists of registered advisers you can approach to see you through to listing.

Visit *http://www.londonstockexchange.com/aim/default. asp* for more information.

Make sure you can agree to the following before approaching investors:

I know what sort of investor I'm looking for. ☐

I have thoroughly researched potential investors and will only approach those who will be interested in my idea. ☐

I have done everything possible to get a contact to make a personal introduction to an investor. ☐

I know my business plan inside out and am confident that when cross-examined by an investor I can answer every question asked of me. ☐

 ## Directory

Below is a selection of sites either packed with advice about raising finance or sites maintained by investors.

http://www.venturesite.co.uk
Register for a fee to advertise your needs to potential investors

http://www.evca.com
European Private Equity and Venture Capital Association: an independent source of info about investment available in Europe

http://www.bvca.co.uk/
British Venture Capital Association: provides a basic guide to raising finance

http://www.vfinance.com/venca.asp
Comprehensive list of VCs from the Venture Capital Resource Library

http://www.vfinance.com/angel.asp
And a list of angels

http://www.lifestyle.co.uk/bea.htm
Links to venture capital firms in the UK

http://www.ventureclub.com/links.html
Links to VCs around the world and details of what they specialise in

http://www.ukbi.co.uk/finance/venture_capital.htm
Comprehensive list of VCs from the UK Centre for Business Incubation. Includes details of their investment criteria and how much they invest on average

http://www.ukbi.co.uk/finance/business_angels.htm
And the same for business angels

http://www.webfanatix.com/
Basic but exhaustive list of links to VC sites

http://mygo.com/dir/Business/Venture_Capital/
Another list of VCs

http://www.toptechnology.co.uk
A useful links section leading to several worthwhile articles on fundraising

http://www.businessbureau-uk.co.uk/account/rais_cap.htm
Advice and info on raising different kinds of finance

http://www.londonstockexchange.com/aim/default.asp
Alternative Investment Market – the lowdown on the first step to the public market for young and growing companies

VC firms

www.epartners.com
www.eventures.co.uk
www.vcapital.com
www.newmediainvest.com
www.alpinvest.nl
www.benchmark.com
www.iii.co.uk
www.e-invest.com
www.gapartners.com
www.apax.co.uk
www.toptechnology.uk
www.marcusventures.com

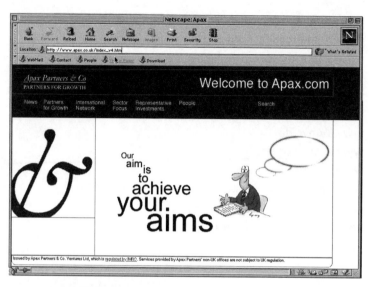

www.capitalexchange.co.uk
www.adventinternational.com
www.amadeuscapital.com
www.artsalliance.co.uk
www.atlasventure.com
www.garage.com
www.entas.com
www.dcfor.com
www.durlacher.com
www.earlybird.de
www.elderstreet.com
www.geocapital.com
www.gle.co.uk

www.innovacom.com
www.kennetcapital.com
www.catfund.com
www.crescendoventures.com
www.quester.co.uk
www.speedventures.com
www.tvmvc.de
www.wellington.de
www.zouk.com
www.thecarlylegroup.com
www.vfinance.com (US directory site)
www.technologieholding.de

Incubators

www.antfactory.com
www.brainspark.com
www.episode1partners.com
www.2becom.com
www.cartezia.com
www.cscape.com
www.ideashub.com
www.esouk.com
www.e-start.com
www.fastfuture.com
www.kpe.com
www.business-incubator.com
www.ectwo.com

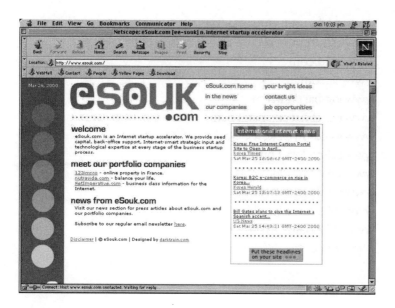

www.lution.com

www.newmediaspark.com

www.ci4net.com

www.protege.co.uk

www.softstartups.com

www.speedventures.com

www.uglyducklings.com

Banks and other sources of funding

www.lloydstsbbusiness.co.uk

www.hsbc.com

www.msdw.com (Morgan Stanley Dean Witter)
www.csfb.com (Credit Suisse First Boston)
www.rsco.com
www.dlj.com
www.ing-barings.com
www.bancbostoncapital.com
www.gs.com (Goldman Sachs)
www.schroders.com
www.db.com (Deutsche Bank)
www.jpmorgan.com
www.ml.com (Merrill Lynch)
www.sbil.co.uk (Salomans Smith Barney)
www.wdr.com (Warburgs)

Entrepreneur Profile | Steve Bowbrick

1. Name
Steve Bowbrick

2. Age
37

3. URL of your business
another.com

4. What is the purpose/nature of your business/website?
Creating fun email addresses for web users.

5. Date your business started
Winter 1998.

6. Is this your first new media venture?
No.

7. Briefly describe your previous business experience and state how useful this was in starting your site

Webmedia – first commercial website design company in the UK. Founded summer 1994, grew to 60 staff, advised and built sites for major consumer brands (Lloyds Bank, TSB, BBC, Consumers Association, RCA, BMG . . .), raised money from Maurice Saatchi's

Megalomedia Group, ran out of road and closed the doors in January 1998.

8. Briefly outline your educational qualifications. Please state which universities/colleges you got these qualifications from.

BA Film and Photography, Polytechnic of Central London 1988
Diplomas in IT and Book Production, A-level textile printing, CSE Grade 1 Mathematics.

9. Were you able to/did you try to raise seed financing from family and friends? If so, how much did you raise?

Seed funding from Jeremy Kerner, friend and founder of Designercity, website design company.

10. Did you have any useful contacts when it came to raising finance? If so, what kind of introductions proved to be the most useful?

Yes. The ones who could move quickly and produce lots of capital.

11. Roughly how much money did you raise in venture capital and was this enough?

£6.25 million. Enough for the first phase of development.

12. How many people were there on your management team?

Four.

13. How useful have you found networking events like First Tuesday and BoobNight?

Good for hiring, less good for capital raising.

14. What would you do differently if you had to start all over again?

Move more quickly in early stages.

15. What do you think are the criteria that have most helped you make a success of your business (e.g. having first mover advantage, a brilliant marketing campaign, bloody-mindedness)?

Great product differentiation – nothing like it in the world. Fit of product to contemporary lifestyles – basically, the product did it!

16. What's been the hardest thing you've had to face since starting your business?

Ragged edge of technology, emotional rollercoaster of delivering a critical communications service round the clock to impatient users.

17. What's the most useful piece of advice you've been given?

'You probably need more money than you think you do.'

18. What's the one piece of advice you wish someone had given you, but didn't?

'Don't over-promise.'

19. Do you believe it's still possible for someone with only a good idea and determination to succeed in new media – or is it all about raising money these days?

First you have only a good idea and determination, then you raise money. Then you use good ideas and determination to deliver, then you raise money ...

20. Are you in profit?

No.

7 Marketing and advertising your site

Some people say that any new dotcom needs to spend 70 per cent of its money on marketing. Others say it's more like 90 per cent. While it's probably true that you need to spend 70 per cent of your *time* on marketing and it's absolutely and unquestionably a fact that website operators need fantastic marketing skills, you don't have to have millions to get noticed.

Any new dotcom needs to spend 70 per cent of its money on marketing.

Marketing is essentially getting a positive message about your site to the greatest number of people. You can do this in several ways: you can use PR (public relations) to get coverage in the press, you can use advertising that can either bang people over their heads or seep slowly into

To market your site effectively you will have to use every technique available, but you should also have a realistic idea about what marketing can do for your site.

their consciousness, and you can use straightforward marketing techniques like handing out leaflets and wearing T-shirts with your logo on them.

It is harder to market a dotcom product than any other product or service you care to mention. This is because not only does dotcom marketing have to get people interested in your site/brand/product/service, it also has to get people to remember your URL. To market your site effectively you will have to use every technique available, but you should also have a realistic idea about what marketing can do for your site.

Most entrepreneurs believe in their site so completely and are so totally immersed in what they're doing that they believe that 'if only the public knew about my wonderful site they would visit in their droves'. This might be true, but even if people hear about your site, visit it and love it there is still no guarantee that they will keep coming back – no matter how vital your service is to their daily life. You must understand that the British public is being bombarded by dotcom advertising right now and they are constantly being tempted to visit new sites. Remembering domain names isn't always easy – just think how often you have visited a great site but can't remember the URL – so you will need a sustained marketing campaign over many months and years to keep the traffic flowing to your site.

This chapter is full of ways to boost your traffic and your

profile – often for no money at all – but you will need to follow almost every bit of advice here (and keep following it) to give your site any chance of long term success.

This chapter is full of ways to boost your traffic and your profile ... but you will need to follow almost every bit of advice here ... to give your site any chance of long term success.

Before you start on your marketing campaign, you need to ask yourself two very important questions and answer them honestly. The first is: is my site ready for the attention? Is my site really the best it can be? If people come will they be disappointed? Will your server crash? Will you be able to fulfil all their orders? The second question is: What do I want to achieve with my marketing campaign? Marketing can help you build brand awareness, get you a lot of press attention, maybe turn you as the founder into the next dotcom celebrity, can increase traffic to your site and change people's opinions. You must set yourself targets now and use the information below to help you reach them.

Free online marketing

Search engines

There are some very basic things that you have to do to get people to notice your site. The first – and possibly the most important – is to get a good ranking for your site on the search engines and directories. Depending on the sort of service you offer you can get anything up to 70 per cent of your traffic from search engines.

There are, as you probably already know, two sorts of search engines: those that are created by humans and those that are created by robots.

The robot-generated search engines rely on information you put in the meta tags and page descriptions of your site to analyse how relevant your site is. The 'bots' are very sophisticated and are very effective at cancelling out sites that put things like 'busty blondes' or 'free money' in their meta tags to get extra traffic. There are plenty of sites that will take you through the best way to present your site to search engines (see the directory at the end of this chapter) and you would be wise to follow their instructions.

It can often take weeks – and several attempts at submitting to a search engine – before your site will get listed. You MUST try and try again and then retry until your site comes up in the first 10 sites in the categories you want to be listed under. Essentially, the best thing to do is to think about what words someone would put into a search engine to find a site like yours. Make sure these words appear in your meta tags and page descriptions.

Directories, that is, search engines compiled by humans, often take the longest to list you. Yahoo is the most famous directory and some webmasters have said they've had to submit their site up to eight times to get someone to look at it. While this is probably unnecessary, you will have to be patient as it takes a long time for someone to visit and rate your site before deciding whether to list you or not.

If, when your site finally gets listed (it can take months and several attempts), you are not happy with its ranking, you must play around with your meta tags, page descriptions and content and resubmit your site. It's time-consuming but worth it. In fact, it is absolutely essential: a high search engine ranking is the best free publicity there is for any new website.

Reciprocal links

The next thing you can do to get your URL in front of people and to encourage them to come to your site is to get links from other sites. If you sell flowerpots, email every other gardening site and ask them to link to yours. In return you create a links section and link to them. No money changes hands, it hardly takes any time to do and it's well worth it because you are only targeting people who you know are interested in your products or services – you're not wasting time and money trying to sell your site to people who aren't interested.

Newsgroups

In the early days of what used to be called the World Wide Web, newsgroups were a very effective way of getting publicity for your site. Newsgroups are essentially message boards where people interested in a certain subject swap ideas and information. Anyone who uses newsgroups simply to sell their site can expect to be spammed by other newsgroup users who may then do their damnedest to make sure you get as much bad publicity as possible. Even quite subtle plugs can receive the most vitriolic of replies, so tread carefully. Use the following sites to identify newsgroups that would be interested to hear about your site, then monitor those newsgroups carefully and only mention your site when it's truly appropriate. Try *http://gort.ucsd.edu/newjour, www.liszt.com* and *www. deja.com* to track down appropriate groups.

Newsgroups are no longer a very effective marketing tool as few web consumers know how to use them. However, those who do can be very influential and may be well worth you targeting. Chat rooms and message boards can also be good places to let people know about your site.

Banner exchanges

Another free way to get your site noticed is by using banner exchange programs. There are lots of them and the directory at the end of this chapter will give you several to sign up to. All you have to do is design a banner that advertises your site, submit it to the program and agree to put an ad for someone else's site on yours. Some services claim they can get you on hundreds of sites for free and others claim you can be on thousands of sites for just a few pounds.

Research for this book has shown that many small sites are disappointed with these programs and no one reported a significant increase in traffic after registering for a banner exchange program. However, banner exchanges aren't really about raising traffic as click-through rates have fallen below the 1 per cent mark. It's also virtually impossible to hold an exchange program to its promises as you're not going to be in a position to monitor whether your banner has appeared on hundreds of sites (possibly only for a few seconds at a time). Unfortunately, it's hard to measure whether banner exchanges have helped raise profiles either, but as it doesn't cost you much it might be worth a try.

Hyperlinks

If you generate a lot of content for your site, a really good trick to get people to notice and visit your site is to get one of the spidering news sites to spider your site. *Newsnow.co.uk* and *moreover.com* are just two services that automatically spider thousands of sites every minute looking for headlines relating to certain fields. These are then aggregated into one newsfeed. What this means in real terms is that a headline from your site might appear in a list with headlines about the same theme/industry/activity from other sites. Each headline is a link which users click on to get the full story on your site.

For the spiders to be able to access your site effectively, you will have to have your headlines as a series of hyperlinks on one page and each story on another page. This might not be the most convenient way for your users to read news, but it's an accepted format that could bring you a lot of traffic if you get spidered by newsnow or moreover.

'Email this to a friend' buttons, bookmarks etc.

There are lots of elements you can include in your site that will encourage people to visit and revisit your site. You can make articles or photos available to email and add an 'Email this to a friend' button. This makes it easy for your users to tell other people about your site. Another tip is to simply have the words 'Bookmark this site now' somewhere on your home page as it encourages people to think of yours as a site they want to return to. If you have a newsletter that you send out, always include a hyperlink to your site and your logo and actively encourage recipients to forward it to friends and colleagues. Sometimes incentivising existing mail list recipients to introduce, say, five people to your site by giving them 5 per cent off their next order can be very effective. Make sure you get your users to endorse you to their friends by any means possible.

Free offline marketing tips

Offline there are also plenty of tricks you can pull for very little outlay. For starters you could incorporate your URL into your logo. This means you only have one image to promote. You then make sure that this image appears on all your stationery and everything else from delivery vehicles to staff T-shirts.

You can start to make your site as press-friendly as possible and create a page where journalists can find out more about your site, your background and where they can register to receive press releases. And if a journalist tells you they're interested in your site or service, keep them interested: quickly make sure they get sent a couple of press releases, even if you weren't planning on sending any out for a while.

Often the cheapest marketing is the most creative, so brainstorm with friends ways you can cheaply reach your target audience. Can you get someone to stand in shopping centres or outside offices with sandwich boards and hand out leaflets? Keep in mind that the most cost-effective marketing is the most targeted: so if you run a site for car enthusiasts, hand out leaflets at race meetings and dealerships, not outside McDonald's.

Volunteer to speak at conferences and events, or to write articles for newsletters: if there is some way that you can make someone else's job easier, that's their best motivation for involving you in an event or project that you can use to promote your site. It also helps to identify you as a voice of authority in your specialist area which can only enhance your credibility and the credibility of your site. It might require a lot of effort, but you should be used to that by now.

PR

Given that PR stands for public relations, it's amazing that PR as a profession has such a bad reputation. Thanks to *Absolutely Fabulous*, PR is seen by many as an industry full of freeloaders who care more about bumping into Lulu than promoting their clients. PR has one major problem with its reputation: everyone thinks it's easy. All you have to do is rattle off a press release, get Möet et Chandon to sponsor a launch and invite a couple of daytime TV presenters and, hey presto, you're in PR, darling.

The truth is that PR is a very strategic activity that requires contacts, imagination and planning, but not always money. It is certainly much cheaper than advertising as a way of getting your message across, but it also tends to be a lot slower and on its own is rarely enough to create a sustained impact on the public consciousness.

Whether or not you attempt to do your PR yourself or you decide to pay professionals to do it for you, there are a few things you should keep in mind. Lisa Hulme runs one of the UK's leading PR agencies specialising in internet projects, big-mouths.com (*www.big-mouths.com*). 'The first thing we always ask a client is what their objectives for the campaign are,' she says. 'No one has yet said to us "We want to make millions of pounds", but if that is their objective they should say so. PR objectives should link directly to your business objectives.'

The most valuable thing a PR agency can give you is contacts. 'Writing a press release isn't exactly rocket science,' says Hulme, 'but actually getting a journalist to write about a site takes a lot more than writing press releases.' Professional PRs know journalists

> *The most valuable thing a PR agency can give you is contacts.*

personally, know their likes, their deadlines and their publication's readership. 'Journalists get swamped by press releases and requests by websites for coverage,' says Hulme, 'so you have to make sure you approach them in the right way.'

You also have to approach different publications in different ways and understand the kinds of stories they are interested in. The trade publication for your target industry may be interested in writing about a fantastic supply deal you've negotiated, but a national newspaper would not. Nationals usually need a consumer angle that is relevant to a big chunk of their readership. One press release certainly does not fit all and in these frenzied times you will have to work hard to make yourself heard above the background noise of thousands of dotcoms screaming for attention. To get your message in the press you are going to have to become very media savvy.

To get your message in the press you are going to have to become very media savvy.
One of the first things you have to accept is that most people couldn't give a toss about you or your site.

One of the first things you have to accept is that most people - and more than most journalists - couldn't give a toss about you or your site. Launching your site might have consumed your every thought for the past year, but most other people couldn't care less. While it's probably worth sending a press release to relevant publications when you launch just to get your name in circulation, don't expect anyone to write about it. What's news to you isn't news to a journalist. The following is a list of events and announcements that will generally guarantee your press release to get no more than a cursory glance: a new launch, staff appointments, an upturn in sales or traffic, a new application for your site.

There are, however, lots of ways you can get journalists to take notice of what you're up to and therefore, you hope, write about you. Basically, you have to hand them a story on a plate. Ways to do this include arranging an online event, perhaps a chat with a well-known player in your field. Getting a celebrity to endorse you is very effective, especially with regional press, although this is not easy.

By all means arrange a party and invite Carol Smillie and the Nolans, but the chances are that they won't turn up.

ClickMango.com got Joanna Lumley onboard by making her a shareholder, guaranteeing her continued endorsement of their service (Star Trek's William Shatner has made millions endorsing internet products in exchange for equity). Unless you have personal contacts with a celebrity or an agent, expect any kind of celebrity association to be an uphill struggle with snooty London agents refusing to return your calls or your emails unless you make exactly the right noises.

A much easier way to generate noise about your site is to conduct a survey. For instance, if you run a site specialising in the recruitment of bar staff, interview a few hundred pint-pullers and ask them how happy they are with their job. With luck you will be able to send out a press release saying something like '70 per cent of bar staff hate their bosses'. You can imagine that the trade publications for the pub trade – and quite a few consumer titles – would be very interested in your survey. Just make sure your URL gets quoted in any coverage.

Another trick is start your own awards programme. Get your readers to vote on a range of subjects related to your site and then get some awards made. Your local engraver might be able to knock you up something, but there is a whole range of marketing merchandise companies that can produce quality gongs at reasonable prices. While an awards ceremony at your local Hilton might go down very well, the chances are that as a new site you won't have the clout to get enough people in the same room together. So phone up the recipients, or the recipients' PAs, tell them they've won and that you'd like to send your representative and a photographer to present them with their award. You then get photographs of senior people in your field photographed with an award bearing your logo – fantastic images for your press pack, and for newspapers and magazines to reprint.

Giving away prizes is another effective way of encouraging the press to write about you. Magazines and newspapers love to offer their readers a chance to do something unique, or at a discount. Think of offers you can make to entice people with: can you give away a certain number of your products for free or at a discount, or can you offer lunch with a well-known figure in your field? Be creative and devise different prizes for different publications.

Never underestimate the power of the freebie.

Once you've concocted your story, you now have to get journalists to write about it. Never underestimate the power of the freebie. Journalists are still impressed when companies give them presents: it's very shallow but extremely effective. Freebies can take the form of an invite to a launch at Old Trafford and a chance to glimpse Manchester United in training, or it can simply be a bar of Cadbury's Dairy Milk that you have put a new wrapper on bearing your logo. You can spend tens of thousands of pounds or just a few pence.

Now you just have to make sure you get your press

release to the right journalist. There's little point sending stuff 'to the editor' as it rarely gets to the right person. Most magazines have a list of personnel somewhere in each issue, so study it and work out the best person to send your info to. It might be worth sending it to several people. Newspapers tend not to have a list of personnel, so in this case the best thing to do is to look at several issues and the journalists' bylines and get a feel for the sorts of stories they're interested in. The next thing to understand about the way the media works is deadlines. Approaching a journalist on deadline day (i.e. the day their magazine goes to press) is a very bad idea. All weekly and monthly publications get busy in the run up to deadlines and calling journalists on these days will seriously irritate them. As a general rule, the day of publication is a good day to get in touch as they will have deadlines behind them and will be planning the next issue. For journalists on national newspapers, earlier in the day is generally better. Online news services are constantly on deadline so it doesn't really matter when you approach them.

Even if you follow all of these steps and execute them with the utmost professionalism, there is still a big chance that your site still won't get written about. This is for two reasons: (a) there are several hundred other dotcoms doing exactly the same thing at the same time, and (b) some of those dotcoms use professional PR agencies.

'People think PR is all about a free lunch,' says big-mouths.com's Victoria McQuade, 'but it's seriously an important part of what we do.' Professional PRs' close and often social relationship with journalists allows them to get to know individual journalists, and the journalist gets to trust PRs when they tell them that product X is worth writing about. 'Contacts are the most valuable thing we can offer a client,' says Lisa Hulme.

Professional PR agencies can also advise you on the timing for your launch or help you organise a party. Good agencies will also help you spend your money wisely. 'We get quite a few requests from potential clients to organise launch parties,' says McQuade. 'We have to tell them that it's really not worth it as the founders can't have serious conversations with journalists who have had five beers. Often it's much better to cherry-pick a couple of journalists and organise a one-to-one lunch.'

Like other professional advisers, some PR agencies may be willing to work for an equity stake with start-ups they really believe in. If you – and they – would rather you paid in cash, you can expect to be charged anywhere between £5,000 and £20,000 a month, plus their expenses. So it's no wonder so many people think they can handle their PR in-house. If you want to find a professional agency, a good tip is to buy magazines like *PR Week* and *Marketing Week* and look for stories about agencies with contacts in your field. Then phone up Directory Enquiries, get the number and get in touch.

Writing a press release

There are some golden rules to follow if you want to write your own press releases. Some of them are so basic it is amazing they have to be mentioned – but even more amazing is the number of completely useless press releases sent out to journalists every day.

1. Your press release must concisely tell journalists what you are announcing. But it must also make it seem exciting. So, 'Fantastic new site for maths students launches' might be accurate but 'Carol Vorderman says smartsums.com is the best site for maths students' is much better 'Nine out ten maths students prefer smartsums.com' is even better.

2. A press release should explain why you have launched your site. In this case it might be because your son had difficulty learning maths and you developed the site to help him: give the journalist a nice personal story to hook into.

3. The press release should also explain how your site works and why it is better than any other site. It is legitimate to use plenty of adjectives, but don't get carried away with claims of 'best ever' that won't stand up to scrutiny.

4. It should give journalists lots of accurate factual information. This must always include dates (of launches, competition deadlines, parties etc.), your URL

and contact details for more information. Ideally you should also include information like 'this site was built for a six figure sum' or clearly state what it cost – it's the sort of thing journalists like to mention.

5. It's a good idea to include an incentive for a journalist to visit your site straight away. This might mean putting juicy information on the site for a limited time, or promising a bottle of wine to the first 50 people to join your mailing list on a certain day.

6. Include a photo, either of your site or of you (obviously this works best if you're either gorgeous or famous – if you're not, be smart and just send a screen grab of your home page).

7. Leave all the boring details – like your professional history, ownership of the company etc. – to an appendix called Notes For Editors. This gives the journalist background information to let him or her write the entire story without getting in touch.

8. Make sure your press release is spellchecked and grammatically correct. If you are sending it out on paper make sure it's on good quality paper with your logo in colour. If you are sending it out as an email put the main body of the press release inside your email. Journalists might not be able to read your attachments and may forget to do so if they have to download them to see them.

Direct marketing and guerrilla marketing

As the prices for conventional advertising skyrocket (see below) more and more sites are using more creative methods of marketing. Graham Hodge, a marketing specialist at eSouk.com, says:

You don't necessarily achieve the best results by burning money on marketing.

'*During the Superbowl 2000 in America, nearly all the ads in the ad break were for dotcom advertisers. One of those companies was a dotcom which had just raised $6 million in venture capital. Within weeks of raising this money it spent $3 million on a minute's worth of advertising in the most expensive ad break of the year. I think it brought them a significant increase in traffic but they had spent their entire marketing budget for the year and couldn't build on it. The moral is that you don't necessarily achieve the best results by burning money on marketing.*'

Given that any marketing campaign has to be prolonged to be effective, you would do well to devise ways of reaching your target audience for the lowest possible price.

Email can be the best tool for marketing on a budget and the secret to stop people from regarding your email as unwanted spam is to make it funny. People love to be sent jokes, funny pictures or .mpeg files of short movies (i.e.

ads). If people think something is funny or relevant, they will often cc it to everyone in their company or address book. Some companies prevent their employees from reading certain sorts of attachments (most commonly .mpegs and .exe files) as they take too long to download and can crash systems, so be warned. A great tip is to come up with a joke of the week that's relevant to your market and send it out to as many people as you can get email addresses for – and don't forget to include a hyperlink back to your site.

When *vault.com* – a US site that encourages employees to bitch about their bosses – launched, they hired a van emblazoned with a piece of gossip about one of the staff to sit outside an office for three days. Everyone in that building looked at the site and the press thought it was such an innovative marketing idea that they wrote about it. The backers of vault.com didn't mind risking a huge bill in parking tickets for all the publicity they got. If you don't want to break the law (although that can be very good for publicity!) you could just hand out leaflets at conventions associated with your target market. Just make sure those leaflets are amusing – it really is the best way to get people to start thinking that your site would be a nice place for them to visit.

Think laterally and creatively about eye-catching stunts you can pull to attract attention – but be careful: a bungled attempt to kidnap a local politician or her cat could make you look like a complete plonker. Be sure that any stunt you decide to stage is something you are 100 per cent confident you can pull off with style. If you end up looking desperate or incompetent your reputation may never recover. Stunts are risky, but daring ones carried out with panache attract press attention, admiration and an increase in traffic.

Advertising

If your site is aimed at the general public you had better prepare yourself for spending millions of pounds on advertising. Newspapers, TV stations and radio stations have started charging dotcom companies more than they charge other sorts of companies for the same exposure. This is because demand from dotcoms is high and many are simply raising more finance to fund expensive campaigns.

If you are spending that kind of cash, it's certain that you'll be getting professionals to design and execute a campaign for you, but you should still have a clear idea of what you want your campaign to achieve. You should also be realistic. A report from America in early 2000 revealed that – despite high levels of dotcom advertising – 25 per cent of adults couldn't name a single website. There is quite simply too much noise, too many conflicting messages and too many similar sites for people who aren't regularly online to tell the difference between sites.

'The current trend in dotcom advertising is on raising awareness,' says eSouk's Graham Hodge. 'A lot of net advertising is very enigmatic and doesn't tell you much about the site or the service. Should dotcoms not be trying harder to convert surfers to shoppers?'

One way of doing this is making much greater use of online advertising. At least you can be sure that the people seeing your ad have access to the internet. There are specialist companies that plan online buying campaigns, but you can also buy your advertising yourself – if you see a site you want to advertise on, ask for their media pack, see how much they charge and what their audience is like – and then haggle.

Some dotcoms have exchanged equity for airtime or space in newspapers. Freeserve Auctions did a deal with regional newspaper group Newsquest swapping advertising space for equity, and C5 took a stake in *rapidinsure.co.uk* in lieu of advertising money. You don't want to do this with any old media company, but strategic alliances such as these two can be enormously fruitful. The reason why dotcoms spend so much on advertising is because it's necessary to keep your brand in view. Many, many companies have spent thousands of pounds on an ad in a national newspaper and waited for the traffic to soar . . . only to be bitterly disappointed. 'I heard a statistic recently,' remembers big-mouths.com's Lisa Hulme, 'that even someone who's really interested in your subject matter needs to see your URL or your logo five times before they will actually go and log on to your site.' It is not enough to advertise once, you need to do it over time and – if you're a B2C site – you will have to do it in print, on TV, online and on radio. Be prepared for your funding to be swallowed up very quickly.

Can you say 'yes' to the following?

Even someone who's really interested in your subject matter needs to see your URL or your logo five times before they will actually go and log on to your site.

I have a top ranking on every search engine. ☐

I may not have a top ranking on every search engine, but I will keep resubmitting my site until I do. ☐

I know who my users are and know which publications I need to write to about my site to hit my target audience. ☐

I have carefully read my target publications for several weeks and have a good idea of the sort of stories they are interested in. ☐

I know which – out of PR, direct marketing or advertising – will be most effective for my site. ☐

Directory

The following sites can help you do everything from set up a banner exchange to plan a million pound advertising campaign.

Help and advice

http://wilsonweb.com/articles/checklist.htm
Twenty-seven ways to promote your website and lots of articles giving tips and advice

http://www.gmarketing.com
Advice on guerrilla marketing techniques

http://www.promotionworld.com/tutorial/index.html
Tutorial on promotion

http://www.businessinsight.org/
Free sample analysis of a marketing strategy for your product or service. Be prepared to answer about 30 questions online about your business to build up a profile of your marketing needs

http://www.web-sitepromotion.com/
Tips and tools for promoting your website

http://netb2b.com/educational_tracks/
Articles on marketing

http://www.clickz.com
Online magazine looking at web advertising, electronic media planning and online marketing

http://www.marketingchallenge.com
Subscription service for access to all articles on net marketing, but some available for free

http://www.marketingtips.com/tipsmnu.html
Advice on promoting your website

http://ecnow.com/internet_Marketing.htm
Marketing tips

Agencies

http://www.webpromotion.co.uk/agencies.htm
List of marketing agencies

http://www.ukbusinessnet.com/prmain.htm?pr/f-prs.htm
List of PR companies

http://www.bluebirds.co.uk/bluebook/media.html
List of PR and ad agencies

http://www.gnash.co.uk
Clients include Lastminute

http://www.big-mouths.com
Specialist internet PR agency

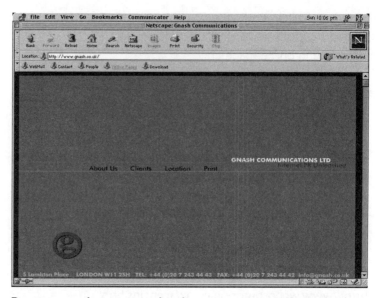

Banner exchanges and other promotional tools

http://www.smartage.com/promote/bannerstudio/
Download a program that helps you design animated banners on your PC

http://www.ukbanners.com/
Banner exchange program 10:8 ratio – you get your banner shown eight times for every 10 times you show someone else's

http://www.searchenginewatch.com
Vital information on getting your site the best possible ranking on search engines

http://www.impressionz.co.uk/
Worldwide exchange program operating a 2:1 ratio

http://www.smartage.com/promote/smartclicks/index2.html
Another 2:1 ratio

http://adnetwork.bcentral.com/
Large international network of banner exchanges. 2:1 ratio. Also
provides free stats

http://uk-banners.wwplus.net/
UK service offering 1:1 ratio banners

http://www.search-it.co.uk/exchange/
Another 1:1 ratio

http://www.uk-find.com/banex/banex.html
An exchange program offering a 5:4 ratio

http://www.nnh.co.uk/ad-net/index2.html
An exchange program offering a 3:2 ratio

http://www.gsponline.com/free1/banner.htm
Dozens of exchange programs to choose from

http://www.groupweb.com/imarketing/banners.htm
List of international banner exchange programs

http://www.adnetworknu.com
Banner ad exposure based on a pyramid selling model

http://www.what-next.com/archives/articles_promotion7.html
A template for making a reciprocal link request

http://www.webpromotion.co.uk/reciprocallinks.htm
List of sites wishing to exchange reciprocal links

http://www.letemknow.com
Puts a referral box on your pages to encourage your fans to evangelise about your service

http://apps3.vantagenet.com/site/linksend.asp
Another 'tell a friend' service

Entrepreneur Profile   Helga St. Blaize

1. Name

Helga St. Blaize

2. Age

39

3. URL of your business

www.ace-quote.com

4. What is the purpose/nature of your business/website?

It is a business to business marketplace for all IT and telecommunications products, services and solutions.

5. Date your business started

June 1999

6. Is this your first new media venture?

Well hey – how many do you need? One is quite enough for me.

7. Briefly describe your previous business experience and state how useful this was in starting your site.

I was a business journalist and editor writing for a number of journals in South Africa on industry news, then returned to London in 1987 when I started specialising in writing about offshore and private finance. Left

London for sunny Cardiff in 1990. Had babies and continued to freelance especially for property journals. This experience has been useful in many respects: as a freelancer working for London-based publishing houses I was aware of the power of the internet before most people. Having babies is always a useful experience and I can thoroughly recommend it to any internet entrepreneur as a way of testing your ability to work around the clock, work on your own and concentrate on four or five different conversations at the same time. Being able to write is always extremely helpful and meant that in our early days I multitasked as PR/content editor/marketing as well as using my knowledge and academic interest in businesses to read, read, read about dotcoms and learn, learn, learn and so have a direct impact on our business strategy. In addition, I would say, having had to interview at a very young and tender age, I am not as intimidated as most people are by financial institutions, banking houses and VCs.

8. Briefly outline your educational qualifications. Please state which universities/colleges you got these qualifications from.

I went to Woldingham School in Surrey and Lavant House School in Sussex, both boarding schools. Did a few A-levels, after which I studied philosophy at Durham University.

9. Were you able to/did you try to raise seed financing from family and friends? If so, how much did you raise?

Absolutely not – both Gary and I have always tried to make sure our families don't get involved in our business even to the extent where we haven't told them anything much about what we do. We don't want to worry them or waste time trying to explain our business to people who couldn't possibly understand what we are.

10. Did you have any useful contacts when it came to raising finance? If so, what kind of introductions proved to be the most useful?

I had one contact, who shall be nameless, who turned out to be extremely influential among a small coterie of unusually wealthy individuals. His support at a rather ropey time helped us and gave us a great deal of confidence in ourselves.

11. Roughly how much money did you raise in venture capital and was this enough?

We invested our own seed capital up to almost £1 million and then raised a further £850,000 in January from Ant Factory, which was enough to get us through another few months. Our aim with Ant Factory was to use them for support and guidance though the next rounds of finance.

12. How many people were there on your management team?

The core two members were always myself and Gary who has 'domain experience' with his IT background, and I am master of all other trades. We also have a COO who is ex-Andersen Consulting and has been extremely useful.

13. How useful have you found networking events like First Tuesday and BoobNight?

In our early days, First Tuesday was useful – I did meet some VCs and was able to practise summoning the courage and confidence to talk about our offering among people who almost spoke the same language. I met Julie Meyer (co-founder of First Tuesday) and Narda Shirley (founder of PR agency Gnash), both of whom have had a lasting impact on my business.

14. What would you do differently if you had to start all over again?

That would be telling – I think the one ingredient we were missing was a great techie (CTO). If I could have found someone like this at the start, it would have made all the difference. So, I suppose putting together a great management team before launching would have been a good idea and might have saved me a few wrinkles.

15. What do you think are the criteria that have most helped you make a success of your business (e.g. having first mover advantage, a brilliant marketing campaign, bloody-mindedness)?

I think just being totally sure that what we are doing is going to succeed has probably been the driving force behind our survival, followed by having first mover advantage and by being very aware of the power of hype – we couldn't afford a great marketing campaign, but we did talk to every journalist who would listen.

16. What's been the hardest thing you've had to face since starting your business?

There was enormous hostility from the IT sector itself and from the IT press. It was felt that we were trying to destroy an already fragile economy. Also, being B2B used to be very unsexy and difficult for the media to understand or to be interested in. Not having enough time for my kids has been really hard too.

17. What's the most useful piece of advice you've been given?

'It's a numbers game.'

18. What's the one piece of advice you wish someone had given you, but didn't?

Change your web-developers. (We have now.)

19. Do you believe it's still possible for someone with only a good idea and determination to succeed in new media – or is it all about raising money these days?

Sadly, a talent for running a business is not enough – a talent for raising money is probably the most useful skill you can possess when starting an internet business. But given the investment climate of the moment, having an amazingly original idea and total determination come close seconds.

20. Are you in profit?

Good lord – what an intimate question! We have only just started to charge for our service but reckon that we could be in profit by the end of this year. As for next year . . .

8 | Running a business

CERTAIN ASPECTS OF RUNNING A business make perfect sense: you need customers, you need to keep them, you need to make a profit, take on staff, pay them etc. etc. Even if you've never run a business before, the basic operations of making money are reasonably practical concepts that most people can get their head round.

However, there is another side to running a business that to most people, frankly, makes no sense at all. It involves virtually anything to do with the government. Sadly, the flipside of ambitious and daring entrepreneurism is deadly dull accounting, due diligence and VAT registration. There are essentially two tasks any company director, MD or CEO has to perform, no matter what size of company he or she operates: administration and stewardship. Of the two, admin is definitely the boring bit and involves everything from book-keeping to compliance with health and safety legislation. Thankfully, if you can afford it, these are the activities it is easiest to outsource, leaving you free to mobilise your workforce, maximise your company's profile and value and generally do what you do best.

This chapter can't tell you the most cost-effective way of handling payroll or the legal complexities of company directors' responsibilities as these things alone would take a decade of study to be able to offer professional advice on. What it does do is tell you what your legal responsibilities are when you start a company, get customers and take on staff. It can also point you in the right direction for finding more information.

Starting a business is extraordinarily time-consuming and you have to be capable of doing three or four things at once. It is entirely possible that you could work solidly 18 hours a day, seven days a week and still have items left on your 'to do' list. And the betting is that those things left on the list will be to do with the tax office or accountancy because, if you don't understand it, it's easy not to bother, especially when dealing with these things takes you away from the cut and thrust of growing your business. Sadly, however, there is no getting away from dealing with the Inland Revenue or other government departments: you can ignore them, but only for a time. And the longer you ignore them, the more it will end up costing you in the future.

What this chapter aims to do is demystify the processes surrounding company law and accountancy, the vagaries of which are used by professional advisers to charge

What this chapter aims to do is demystify the processes surrounding company law and accountancy, the vagaries of which are used by professional advisers to charge hundreds of pounds an hour.

hundreds of pounds an hour. The good news is that there are some excellent sites containing comprehensive information – most of which is available for free – to help you. The government, bless 'em, also has a range of helplines and information packs which are there to help new employers get to grips with their responsibilities. When letters arrive in Inland Revenue envelopes you have nothing to fear. Honest.

Getting help

Shelling out money on professional advice often seems – and often is – a waste of money in the very early days of a business. There isn't much that's urgent and the stuff that is can easily be dealt with by someone with half a brain. However, if you are serious about growing a large company with large profits, it makes sense to start off as you mean to carry on. You will almost certainly need professional advice from an accountant and a solicitor to help you set up your company and your books in such a way as to impress investors and future partners.

While you might not immediately need someone to set up a payroll for you or incorporate you as a limited company, it makes sense to start talking to advisers early on. Ask around for recommendations for a good company lawyer, management consultant and a helpful accountant. Tell them what you're up to and get them interested in your business so that when something comes up that you can't deal with, they're only a phone call away. This relationship building will guarantee them your business in future months and gives you the safety net you need. The government operates a scheme called 'Lawyers for your Business' which provides you with a free legal consultation from participating solicitors for a minimum of 30 minutes. Contact the Law Society on 020 7405 9075 for details of a solicitor in your area.

In addition there are various schemes operated by the Chamber of Commerce and organisations like Business Link that can put you in touch with a small business advisor for free, sometimes for the whole of your first year in business. Schemes vary wildly from area to area, so use the links in the directory at the end of this chapter to find out what's available near you. Your other port of call for advice is your bank. Many high street branches have small business advisors who have good local contacts with accountants, lawyers and other advisors.

Limited company status

For most people starting a new company there are three options: operating as a sole trader, partnership or limited company. You could also become a public limited company, but if you are choosing this route you will already have taken legal advice far more detailed than a book like this can offer you.

Operating either as a sole trader or a partnership essentially means you are self-employed. Legally, you must inform the Inland Revenue that you are now self-employed and keep a record of your income and your outgoings. You will automatically be sent all the forms you need and, at the appropriate time of the year, a tax return which you need to fill in accurately and return to the tax office by the due date. It isn't any more scary than that. Any high street accountant can do your tax return for you, but it isn't necessary. The hard part is making sure you put a percentage of your income aside to pay your tax bill! If you are in a partnership it is wise to draw up a legal contract between partners, but it is not a mandatory requirement.

For companies serious about raising finance and entering the world of big money, it is advisable to become a limited company. This is relatively straightforward, but it comes with additional responsibilities.

So what are the benefits of incorporation (the term used for establishing yourself as a limited company)? The most important one is limited liability. This means that the financial liability of the shareholders is limited to the amount they have paid for their shares. So if your company were to incur debts, the individual shareholders – i.e. you and your partners – aren't legally bound to meet those debts.

Another benefit is that it formally separates ownership from control. While initially it is likely that the founders will wholly own and operate the company, when investment is made it is possible to issue shares to an investor which do not give control away. However it is likely that investors – especially those coming in at later rounds of finance – will want shares with preferential rights attached to them. There are other benefits too which are detailed at the Companies House site (*www.companieshouse.org.uk*), but a hidden benefit that never really gets mentioned is that it makes you look like you are serious about your business. Being a limited company gives you stature among associates that makes the hassle of incorporation well worth it.

There are, of course, additional responsibilities associated with being a director or secretary of a limited company that are set out in law. There are also some administrative headaches attached to running limited companies. Let's start with the headaches first . . .

Directors of limited companies, when they take earnings from the company, must be on the company's payroll. This means that not only will tax and National Insurance contributions (NICs) be taken out at source, but in addition you will have to pay employers' NICs (typically an additional 12 per cent). Limited companies also have to pay corporation tax on their profits (after all overheads, including salaries, have been deducted) and this is variable between 20 per cent and 32.5 per cent depending on the size of your profits (if you were operating as a sole trader you would be paying income tax of between 25 per cent and 40 per cent on those profits).

Responsibilities mostly relate to the keeping of accounts and giving a copy of those accounts to Companies House each year. This can significantly increase time and money spent on accountancy. There are also legal guidelines that have to be adhered to when issuing shares, and if you go bankrupt it can affect future directorships you might be offered. The duties of directors include slightly ambiguous things like being well behaved, diligent and honest, and undertaking not to defraud someone or trade when knowingly insolvent or to deceive shareholders. The details of these responsibilities are all available on the Companies House website.

Incorporating a company isn't very hard and needn't be expensive unless you get an accountant to do the paperwork for you. All you need to do is visit the Companies House website and find out exactly what documents you require (these include the Articles of Association and the Memorandum of Association). Your 'Mem & Art', as lawyers and accountants refer to them, register the names of the directors and company secretary, as well as setting out the objectives of the company. These can be purchased from a legal stationers for little more than £10, then you need to fill them in, get them witnessed by a solicitor (who may charge you a nominal amount for his/her trouble) and send the documents to Companies

House along with a small fee. After a few weeks you will be sent a Certificate of Incorporation with your Company Number on it which you should include on your headed notepaper in future. It is also possible to buy an existing company which, if you have an accountant taking care of matters for you, usually works out cheaper.

There are some restrictions on the names you can use – certain words like 'group' or 'royal' need certain certification – but you can check to see if the name you want is available – you guessed it – on the Companies House website.

VAT

VAT (value added tax) is a tax which is added to most purchases at the rate of 17.5 per cent. This is a tax which other people will add to goods you purchase and that you can add to goods you sell. What's the point of that then? Well, if you are charged more for VAT than you yourself charge, you can claim the difference back from the VAT office. The other advantage is that you can account for your VAT separately and earn interest on monies collected before handing them over to the Inland Revenue. This benefit does require added time and effort in accountancy, however. The real advantage though, is that it makes you look pukka in the eyes of your trading partners (it's a bit embarrassing when people ask for your VAT registration

Starting your own business?

Here are the forms and information you need!

Inland Revenue

'Working together for you'

number and you have to say 'Er, we don't have one').

Registering for VAT is optional if your turnover is below £52,000 per annum. As soon as you reasonably expect your turnover to hit that benchmark you are required by law to register for VAT. It is remarkably simple: just call your local VAT office (number in your local telephone directory) and tell them you want to register. They'll send you a form (VAT 1) to fill in, you return it and in a couple of weeks you have a VAT number to put on your invoices. Check out *www.hmce. gov.uk/bus/vat/index.htm* for more information.

If you are an e-commerce site selling VAT-able goods to overseas customers, you will need specialist advice about invoicing those customers. It's a headache shared by all e-commerce traders, some of whom have been lobbying for a simplification of VAT rules across international boundaries.

Employer's responsibilities

If your plans work out, you should be an employer before too long. This can be frightening for entrepreneurs who have willingly taken risks and know that a downturn may only be weeks, or maybe only days, away. When you take on staff you will feel responsible for making sure their rent gets paid and that your company continues to be solvent – suddenly you feel responsible to minimise risk. Taking on staff – i.e. taking people away from stable employment – to join a new (and therefore insecure) company is a big step, and one of the hardest things to get right. If you do find this additionally stressful, you must tell yourself that you're not jeopardising their future, but instead congratulate yourself for giving them the best opportunity of their careers – to come in at the ground level of a new company is a chance many people would kill for.

The 'stewardship' side of recruitment and management will be tackled in the next chapter, but here we will deal with the administration side. The first thing you should do is put down this book and take a look at *www.dti.gov.uk/ COMMS/employ/index.htm*. It doesn't give much detail, but this well designed Department of Trade and Industry site simply and clearly outlines your responsibilities. There is also a new employers' helpline operated by the Inland Revenue which is open till 8pm on 0845 60 70 143. If you call it you will be sent a New Employer's Starter Pack which contains enough documents to take on your first couple of members of staff. If you find it really com- plicated, someone from the Business Support Team at your local Inland Revenue office will come to visit you to talk you through the forms. In addition to this, the Inland

Revenue organises free seminars for people operating payrolls, covering everything from the payment of Statutory Sick Pay to the basics of employment law. You should also get hold of form CWL1 from the Inland Revenue called Starting Your Own Business. ACAS – the employment conciliation service – also provides advice for new employers. Other sources of advice can be found through (in England) Business Link on 0345 567765, (in Wales) Business Connect on 0345 969798 and (in Scotland) Scottish Business Shops on 0800 787878 all of which will be able to provide you with a very useful booklet called 'Employing Staff – A Guide To Regulatory Requirements'.

Briefly, your responsibilities as an employer are to pay your employees, to pay their tax and NICs, to pay employers' NICs, to abide by health and safety legislation and to issue a contract of employment within two months of someone joining your company. In addition, you will have responsibilities in regard to the minimum wage, equal opportunities, the hours and conditions of work and the payment of statutory sick and maternity pay.

When you take on your first employee, obtain their P45 (or if they don't have one they can fill in a P46 form which is in your Starter Pack) and tell the Inland Revenue. When you pay them, you must deduct the necessary tax and NI and submit the due contributions to the Inland Revenue each month or quarter. You must also give your employee a pay slip detailing the deductions. Leaflet CWG1, 'An

Employers Quick Guide to Pay As You Earn and National Insurance Contributions', will help you.

Any member of staff you intend to employ permanently must be given a contract of employment within two months of joining your company. This is a fairly standard but important legal document which a solicitor can draw up for you. Sites such as *www.desktoplawyer.net* produce standard documents for situations like this that you can easily adapt for your own requirements, and at a fraction of the cost of using a traditional solicitor. An employment contract should outline an employee's job title, salary, entitlement to bonuses/share options, place of work, hours of work, notice period etc. Sometime in 2001, every employer will be legally obliged to run a pension scheme (although it will not be compulsory for employers to make additional contributions).

Other key responsibilities

When you move into offices, there will be additional regulations that you as an employer will need to be aware of. These generally fall under the banner of health and safety and require you to ensure that your offices are fit for the work you are asking people to do. You will need to take out some kind of employers' liability insurance which gives you protection if something happens to one of your staff while on your premises. If you have members of the public

– or indeed anyone – visiting your place of work you will also need public liability insurance. Many insurance firms offer a package deal for new and small businesses that includes both these requirements and things like contents insurance for one price. It can be surprisingly cheap and shouldn't cost you more than £1,000 a year if your company stays small.

As your company grows – and most successful dotcoms seem to grow at exponential rates – it is hard to remember to keep on top of all your responsibilities which include everything from making sure you have a first aider on the staff to making sure fire exits are clearly marked to paying your Corporation Tax and filing your accounts with Companies House. But these duties are important and there is no excuse for not taking them seriously. There are also financial and legal penalties if you don't attend to them.

Basic book-keeping

Book-keeping has a bad reputation. Everyone thinks it's dull. Actually, it is extremely tedious but . . . it is also curiously rewarding. Keeping good books, and keeping good book-keeping habits, can teach you a lot about how your business is doing. It's also a legal obligation.

Essentially, book-keeping is just keeping a record of your income and your outgoings. If you buy something, you make a note of it, and if someone buys something from you, you make a note of it. Unfortunately it's not quite *that* simple, and gets more complicated if you are registered for VAT or incorporated. But the more regularly to attend to your books, the less daunting it will be and the less trouble you're likely to get into. If possible, set aside a designated hour a week for totting up your receipts and invoices rather than letting a mountain of paperwork build up. Neglecting your books could cost you dearly in the long term and will take up more of your time as you come to the end of the accounting year.

For non-registered, non-incorporated businesses, you can keep your accounts in a simple analysis (cash) book from any stationers. But seeing as you're a net company with technical savvy, it makes sense to start a couple of spreadsheets – one for sales and one for expenses – each month.

VAT registered businesses and limited companies need to keep slightly more information and details on this: plenty of advice is available from the websites listed in the directory at the end of this chapter in much greater detail than it's possible to go into here.

Other legal responsibilities

Companies that operate on the net are still subject to the same laws other real world companies are bound by.

Customers still have rights to refunds for faulty goods bought in good faith from your site and you still can't make false claims about other people's sites, services or products.

Libel laws are something all website operators should be mindful of, as any defamatory statement made on the web is just as liable for prosecution as one made in print. Libel, in essence, is saying something about someone that (a) isn't true and (b) brings their reputation into disrepute. It is not libellous to say something that isn't true (you can't be sued for saying someone wore a blue dress when they were wearing a red one, for instance), nor is it libellous to publish something on your site which 'lowers someone in the eyes of their peers' – a legal definition – if it is accurate.

Many websites are guilty of the most outrageous breaches of libel law because they do not monitor their chat rooms and message boards which contain unfounded allegations written by users. There are many vexed discussions taking place in legal circles about the responsibilities of webmasters and content editors in respect to these matters. As yet, the number of cases brought are few as the worst offenders tend to be fan sites with no real world counterpart. If you are a limited company, or just a responsible trader, it will be easy for a solicitor to find you to sue you.

Current thinking on libel on the web is polarised: you should either not manage your message boards or chat rooms at all and make it quite clear they are unmonitored and your company in no way endorses any opinions expressed on those pages, or you read everything before it is put up. Any half-way house, the argument goes, means that you are aware of people saying defamatory things but doing nothing to stop it.

However, neither of the extreme options offers any satisfactory defence in law: just because you were not aware of a defamatory statement made on your site does not prevent you from prosecution, neither does 'trying to do the right thing' (i.e. reading everything and putting in a few 'allegedlys') if the statement is inherently untrue and damaging.

Libel is one of the few areas of law where there is no entitlement to legal aid. And if you are found guilty, your accuser can seek damages not just from your company but also from you personally. There have been cases where ISPs have been sued for libel because the libellous statement was held on one of their servers. The other thing you should know about libel is that it is the jury – not the judge – that sets the level of damages, and traditionally juries award much bigger damages than legal professionals.

Now that you're completely scared, what can you do? The first thing is to be cautious. Ask yourself if it is entirely necessary for you to include that barbed but possibly libellous comment on your site. If you're worried, edit it judiciously or leave it out. Alternatively you could get yourself some libel insurance which most brokers will be able to arrange for you. If you have a lawyer, it is worth expressing your concerns and getting some advice.

There isn't a set of questions for this chapter for a very good reason: there is no test to measure your readiness or threshold to demonstrate your excellence this time: you just have to do it.

Directory

The following sites should help you find practical advice on everything from employment law to paying your VAT.

Starting-up

http://finance.uk.yahoo.com/glossary.html
Business terminology explained

www.enterprisezone.org.uk
A comprehensive links directory for small businesses in the UK. Get sales and marketing information, and advice on starting-up, human resources, training, finances and legal matters

http://www.ibm.com/e-business/what/how/index.html
Tips on how to set up your e-commerce business from targeting your customers to implementing the technology

www.new-business.co.uk
Very useful site for people running new businesses

www.dti.gov.uk/COMMS/business.index.htm
The government sets out your obligations here

Organisations

http://www.inlandrevenue.gov.uk/home.htm
Official government site with advice and information. Download leaflets and booklets

www.tax.org.uk/
Handy tax tips from the Chartered Institute of Taxation

www.hmce.gov.uk/bus/vat/index.html
VAT explained

www.companies-house.org.uk
Order forms, ask questions via email – usually next day response. Limited companies index (Mon to Fri 8am to 8pm) and all the guidance booklets online

http://www.britishchambers.org.uk
Links to all Chambers of Commerce in the UK and Ireland with a 'Find your Chamber' service

www.businesslink.co.uk/links/index.htm
Information and advice for businesses from starting up to selling and marketing. Can help you find your local office (England)

www.iba.org.uk
The Institute of Business Advisors was set up to assist the start-up and stimulate the growth of small and medium-sized enterprises

www.iba.org.uk/branch.htm
List of branches in the UK

http://www.isbauk.org
Institute of Small Business Affairs

http://www.icaewfirms.co.uk
Institute of Chartered Accountants of England and Wales provides a searchable (by location and specialist area) list of accountants

http://www.icas.org.uk/
Institute of Chartered Accountants of Scotland

http://www.acca.org.uk
Association of Chartered Certified Accountants

http://www.aat.co.uk
Association of Accounting Technicians

http://www.cima.org.uk
Chartered Institute of Management Accountants

http://www.cim.co.uk
Chartered Institute of Marketing

http://www.ukbi.co.uk/finance/support.htm
Extensive list of support agencies from the UK Centre for Business Incubation

http://www.martex.co.uk/sites.htm
Links directory of UK trade associations, from osteopathy to racehorse training

Help and advice

http://www.ecommercetimes.com/small_business/
Tips and features on small business e-commerce ventures from strategy to branding

www.nmkadapt.co.uk/business_support/default.cfm
Ask Sian the agony aunt business questions. Also legal information and small business essentials including FAQs – VAT, patenting and setting up a payroll

www.businessbureau-uk.co.uk/
Top tips for any small business – including what to put in a business plan, preparing accounts, employment rights and marketing

http://edge.lowe.org/
Lots of help for entrepreneurs from Entrepreneurial Edge, including tips on recruiting staff and marketing

http://www.excite.iii.co.uk/tax/?type=knowledge&subtype=14
Simple and brief guide to UK tax system

http://www.altosnet.com/EntrepreneurshipAtoZ/eaz38.1.htm
Take a free online course in entrepreneurship

http://www.solobiz.com
Valuable advice and hints on starting a business

http://www.bird-online.co.uk/
Offers a broad range of business related information including details of events, a database of consultants and business diagnoses. Also searchable database of useful links

http://www.company-services.co.uk
Advice for people wanting to set up a limited company

http://www.businesslink.co.uk
A good source of general companies advice

http://www.instant-search.com
Here you can do a quick search on companies and names

http://www.formationsdirect.ltd.uk
More help on forming a company

http://www.enterprisezone.org.uk
General advice on getting going

Useful services

http://www.ukbusinessnet.com/cdb/content-home.htm
List of business to business services in the UK from printing to legal

www.lawrights.co.uk
Buy basic employment contracts, confidentiality and partnership agreements to your specification

www.netaccounts.com
Online accountancy advice

www.patent.gov.uk
The Patent Office's official resource for info on copyright matters

www.emplaw.co.uk
This isn't the most useful site in the world, but it does contain details of solicitors specialising in employment law which are searchable by area

www.desktoplawyer.net
A range of off the shelf contracts to download for relatively low fees

Banks

The following banks have good online resources for businesses

http://www.barclays.com
http://www.flemings.com/premier
http://www.natwest.com

Entrepreneur Profile | Geraldine Billam

1. Name
Geraldine Billam

2. Age
34

3. URL of your business
www.the-bullet.com

4. What is the purpose/nature of your business/website?
Alternative media portal.

5. Date your business started
August 1999.

6. Is this your first new media venture?
Yes.

7. Briefly describe your previous business experience and state how useful this was in starting your site.

I ran my own design company. Before that I worked for Islington Council – in a position completely unrelated to new media (Housing Benefits!).

8. Briefly outline your educational qualifications. Please state which universities/colleges you got these qualifications from.

A-levels in chemistry, physics, maths and art. BTEC Professional Development, Kingsway College.

9. Were you able to/did you try to raise seed financing from family and friends? If so, how much did you raise?

No.

10. Did you have any useful contacts when it came to raising finance? If so, what kind of introductions proved to be the most useful?

None.

11. Roughly how much money did you raise in venture capital and was this enough?

Six figures but still seeking finance.

12. How many people were there on your management team?

Two.

13. How useful have you found networking events like First Tuesday and BoobNight?

Meat markets – We Gather (for women entrepreneurs) was much more organised and helpful.

14. **What would you do differently if you had to start all over again?**

Have a rich family!

15. **What do you think are the criteria that have most helped you make a success of your business (e.g. having first mover advantage, a brilliant marketing campaign, bloody-mindedness)?**

Determination, bloody hard work, good contacts (with our target industries), fantastic content.

16. **What's been the hardest thing you've had to face since starting your business?**

Third parties not meeting their commitments.

17. **What's the most useful piece of advice you've been given?**

Don't expect to get any breaks.

18. **What's the one piece of advice you wish someone had given you, but didn't?**

Everything takes longer and costs more than you expect (a bit like DIY).

19. **Do you believe it's still possible for someone with only a good idea and determination to succeed in new media – or is it all about raising money these days?**

If they have the technological background to make it happen

themselves, then yes. Otherwise I think it may be too late to 'have a go' without financial backing.

20. Are you in profit?

Depends what you mean by profit – we don't owe any money – but we are expanding rapidly, so we're spending money faster than we're making it at the moment.

9 Possible problems

Here is an absolute rule about the internet: any entrepreneur who takes a second to congratulate himself will be overtaken by a rival. Success brings its own pressures, responsibilities and problems.

HERE IS AN ABSOLUTE RULE ABOUT the internet: any entrepreneur who takes a second to congratulate himself will be overtaken by a rival. Getting your site built and your company funded does not mean you have a successful e-business. To get one of those, you still have a few more mountains to climb.

Success brings its own pressures, responsibilities and problems. On paper you might have planned to hire someone to perform a certain job that would increase your income by 20 per cent. In reality it takes you four months to find the right person, who has to give three months' notice, by which time you've lost so much ground to rivals that the 20 per cent increase in profits is unrealistic and not enough anyway.

In the rapidly changing world of the internet, keeping

on top is hard, as is the day-to-day management of a company when your business is expanding in six directions at once. Here are some of the common problems e-entrepreneurs face.

Time management

Time is your greatest enemy. People who run content-rich sites that need daily maintenance can quite easily spend their every waking hour updating their site. It's the single biggest drawback of launching a website before securing funding: while you are busy running your site a rival is out there raising millions on a full-time basis and arranging meetings with partners you haven't got time to see.

When you are doing everything from updating your site to recruiting staff to arguing with the printers about your business cards to dealing with the Inland Revenue to meeting with the bank to handing out leaflets at trade fairs to managing every other tiny detail, it is absolutely vital that you develop excellent time management skills.

You have to learn to prioritise tasks and make compromises every day.

You have to learn to prioritise tasks and make compromises every day. When you need to go to a meeting, for example, your site will get neglected or the books won't get updated. For this reason, larger management teams that can delegate duties (and respect each others' decisions) can usually move faster. If you are on your own or working with one other person it is a good idea to enlist new people to your team to work with you rather than under you. Maybe you need a great strategist to move the company forward while improving your site, or maybe you need an assistant who can handle the admin while you scratch backs with strategic partners. Free up as much spare time as you can by outsourcing as many tasks as possible. Everything from payroll to getting your office cleaned can be handled by an outside company.

The reason for this is that time outside your brain and outside your office is moving faster than you think. While you immerse yourself in your site and your company, elsewhere the very fact that you have launched your site has made rivals and potential rivals think that they can do better. As soon as you start to get even slightly successful you will find that other companies will be coming after you.

Even if you are lucky and you somehow manage to avoid the nightmare of fierce competition, you will find that the market changes under your feet. Ideas that were developed for the web in 1999 suddenly found they couldn't secure the next round of funding in 2000 unless they had negotiated WAP distribution or had developed an application for digital TV. This industry moves so fast and is powered by insecure money men who throw their funds into whatever is fashionable – it can be a mammoth task pandering to the whim of the day.

Staying focused

As a general rule you should ignore whims of the day. To succeed you will need to be disciplined and that doesn't just mean avoiding hangovers and daytime TV. A disciplined entrepreneur is not swayed by the latest fad. If you don't believe that your site has a WAP application or e-commerce slant – and you are sure of this – then don't waste your time building one or even planning one. Stay true to your idea, stick to your guns and don't lose your focus just because someone with an intergalactic messaging system

To succeed you will need to be disciplined and that doesn't just mean avoiding hangovers and daytime TV.

just raised a billion in venture capital. Many entrepreneurs will tell you, however, that the biggest mistake they made was not thinking big enough; building a little business only to have it consumed or bullied by a big business is not a smart thing to do. Keep an open mind but keep your focus.

 ## Looking after your health

People who work hard need to take care of themselves. If you spend seven days a week working, activities like going to the supermarket or the gym become either unnecessary or inconvenient. You end up not exercising and eating junk food because even if you make it to the supermarket your brain is incapable of switching off work and remembering to get anything other than two bags of pasta and a selection of stir-in sauces.

Of course, it's not just your physical health that can suffer, but also your emotional health. Time spent with your business is time you used to spend with your partner, friends or just in front of the TV. While you will almost certainly have to sacrifice some quality in your relationships and your diet, it's vital that you don't let your business take over, otherwise you won't have the energy to carry on, or the emotional support to see you through the tough times.

One London-based entrepreneur says:

'I found it impossible to get any exercise at all. But then I realised one day when I was going through the books that I was spending £100 a week in couriers picking up and delivering items within a mile of my house. I realised it would be much quicker if I went out and picked up packages myself. In London there are so many parks that a brisk walk or cycle was a pleasure and became a necessary part of my day.'

Not everyone is capable of being their own courier, but if there are ways you can build exercise into your day you will stay fit and have more energy.

It is also virtually impossible for people running early stage companies to take a holiday. The most you can hope for is a long weekend with your laptop and mobile phone permanently switched on! So you need to build in power-breaks. This means getting maximum relaxation in the minimum amount of time. Massages are good, as is curling up with a good book and a glass of wine. Find some activity that forces you to slow down, breathe deeply and think about something – anything – other than your business for the odd half hour (or if you're lucky or desperate, half a day).

Entrepreneurs interviewed for this book had few tips for keeping heart and soul together and all recognised it was a serious problem. Advice ranged from taking office space in a building with a gym in the basement to playing squash with the rest of the management team once a week. The only tip anyone could come up with for eating well was getting a wife! 'I can never get to the supermarket so there is never anything for breakfast and as I'm still at the office in the evening we usually get pizza delivered to our desks,' said the manager of an online publishing company. 'My skin hasn't been this bad since I was a teenager.'

While your diet and hamstrings might not be a top priority as you launch your business, if you don't find some routine for looking after yourself, you will slowly lose stamina and vitality – two essential ingredients for success. So take a vitamin supplement, keep a bowl of fruit on your desk and walk instead of hopping on the bus.

Building a team

One of the fascinating facts that emerged during the research for this book was that almost every entrepreneur had difficulty in recruiting the right staff. There is a serious skill shortage in new media, with few people having directly relevant experience. And with the number of internet companies mushrooming, so are incidences of poaching. Staff with more than six months' experience in an internet company can often add thousands of pounds to their take-home pay by jumping ship.

One of the fascinating facts that emerged during the research for this book was that almost every entrepreneur had difficulty in recruiting the right staff.

'People have become incredibly money

motivated,' said one employer. 'I know of several people who have left equity on the table at one company for equity at another company simply because they thought their new employer would IPO more quickly.'

Another entrepreneur found that recruitment took up much more of her time than she had budgeted for: 'We started using a recruitment agency to save time even though we hadn't budgeted for their fees. But even some of the people the agency brought in left before their six month review.'

There are many things you will have to do in order to recruit and hold on to a winning team. You will certainly need to offer them stock options: they will need to feel that working for your company is their best chance of paying off their mortgage, buying a loft apartment in Clerkenwell or becoming a millionaire themselves. You should expect to have to make stock options available to your first 20 staff, if not all of them, and allow for between 10 and 20 per cent of your company to be in employees' hands. Everyone working for an internet start-up expects this. You cannot view it as a perk. They are taking a risk in joining a new company and you must reward this risk.

You must not see this as giving away equity: staff with stock options are more motivated to work extra hours, muck in at times of stress and evangelise about your site when they meet clients and therefore add tremendous value to your business. Nevertheless, this still isn't enough in the current climate. An American entrepreneur based in the fevered Silicon Valley has found she needed to do more to keep hold of her staff: 'We have told our sales staff that we will buy the most successful of them a BMW at the end of the year,' she says. 'We also take all our staff out to lunch on Wednesdays and take them away for weekends and do activities together like paintballing.' This, she explains, is simply to make them think twice about jumping ship when a rival offers them more equity. 'Believe me, we're a start-up and funds are tight, but we're richer for spending money like this.'

If you have never managed staff before, it might be worth getting some training or at least reading some management books to give you some guidance. The biggest reason for people leaving start-ups before they can cash in their chips is because they felt 'out of the loop.' Sometimes founders are so busy raising more money or setting up branches in other countries that they forget to keep their team up to speed. Remember to thank your staff for doing their job well. Also remember that staff who are keen to join a start-up probably have some entrepreneurial ambitions themselves, so if they come up with a good idea, let them take the (financial) credit for it.

When you are looking for new staff, don't just look at people with directly relevant work experience. Not only will someone with internet experience cost you more in the salary department, but experience isn't as relevant in a new industry. 'The important thing to look for is transferable skills,' says the director of one recruitment agency. 'If someone can sell for a print publication they can sell for a website, but they will need training.' Smart people can quickly learn new software, especially if they are encouraged to do so, so don't rule out potential employees just because they don't have a working knowledge of HTML. And don't stop training your staff. As technology moves on it could leave you stranded if your company doesn't understand it. Staff who are well trained generally feel more capable and work harder and accomplish more.

Keeping a team together

When a business starts to grow management teams can grow apart. And a management team at war is destined for destitution. The single biggest reason for founding partners to fall out is lack of communication. While each of you is out fighting for different parts of the business, sometimes the common goal may start to be interpreted differently. Each thinks the other doesn't understand their role, or doesn't appreciate the remarkable deal they just pulled off. If someone doesn't pull their weight it causes terminal resentment, especially when the weak or lazy partner has an equal equity stake in the company.

One solicitor had this piece of advice for management teams: 'Draw up contracts.' Of course a solicitor would say this, as this is the sort of work that puts his children through university, but some kind of formal agreement may be worth considering. At any rate, make sure you all know what you as individuals are responsible for and that you all appreciate what the others add to the mix. Make sure you know what will happen if someone wants to pull out, or if the rest of you want to get rid of someone else. Whatever you do, regular meetings are essential to keep each other updated on progress and problems.

Technology

One of the biggest headaches suffered by e-entrepreneurs has been to do with relying on new and untried technology. Imagine that your servers go down, or your entire system is infected with a virus. Even technology that works perfectly can prove problematic: suddenly you will have customers getting in touch 24 hours a day who want immediate answers.

There is a very good reason why investors look at management teams to make sure you have a competent CTO (chief technological officer): if something goes wrong it is important to have someone who can fix the problem ASAP. But not all problems are fixable. 'The web itself can be very unstable,' muses one CEO who occasionally notices inexplicable downturns in traffic. 'Some days we only got half of our normal visitors and we couldn't work out why. After some investigation it actually turned out that a phone cable somewhere near Nottingham had been severed by road builders which had halved the capacity of people able to reach our server. Another time a power cut where our server was held shut the site down for over six hours.'

For every live chat ever hosted, there has been a webmaster with nails chewed to the quick and for every new piece of software there are a hundred users who find faults beta tests didn't reveal. 'The technology we're relying on is all so new, and as more and more people go online it slows the whole system down, consumers get frustrated waiting for pages to download and we all get a bad name,' says the CTO of an e-commerce operation.

In other cases, people have planned the evolution of their company based on the promises of software firms or press reports that hailed the arrival of a new application which took six months longer than expected to deliver. The biggest problem most people reported was the pace of change: as soon as they had invested in one system, a better or cheaper one became available. The best advice anyone had to offer was 'be smart, but be lucky.'

The problems of success

Apart from your friends becoming so jealous of you that they can no longer look you in the eye, success for an e-business can often bring unforeseen problems. For e-commerce companies, these are often related to logistics, i.e. their ability to deliver goods. If you are lucky you will be swamped with orders for your competitively priced goods. But what happens if you set your prices low as a temporary measure to attract traffic, and suddenly you have thousands of people snapping something up at a price that means you can't make a profit? This is the least of your problems: have you got a good enough relationship with your supplier to increase your order? And have you got a courier who can suddenly cope with delivering many more orders than he was expecting without charging you more, because he knows you're in a tight spot?

And then what happens if goods are faulty? Will you pick them up at no cost to the consumer? Will there be a 24 hour helpline customers can call? Do you have a customer relations manager who can handle your relationships with customers without whom you cannot grow your business? These are all questions you will need to answer.

The other major problem with success is that someone will try to follow in your footsteps. That sleeping dinosaur of a company whose clients you thought you could steal may suddenly wake up and throw money and power into destroying your business. You must be prepared for rivals to come at you with everything they've got. You will be irrationally enraged by their actions – after all, they're threatening your baby – but you must calm down enough to realise that rivals can be good for business.

A rival can help a business define itself. Instead of simply selling garden furniture, which has provided you with a nice business up until now, you might realise that specialising in stainless steel chairs to West London media types is a better business. It enables you to better target your customers, deliver better products and charge a premium for your trendy service. Meanwhile your rival carries on selling unfashionable sun loungers with floral patterns to the masses and spends a fortune on logistics and advertising!

A competent, monied rival is just about the scariest thing a new company can face, but a rival can help you see what you're not, can force you to define your proposition and can help you establish a brand.

> *A competent, monied rival is just about the scariest thing a new company can face.*

Promises, promises

No matter how carefully prepared your business plan is, it will be out of date within a few months. Promises you made in January will be impossible to deliver in February, meanwhile you have investors and clients expecting you to deliver what you promised. Managing the expectations of your investors, your clients and your staff is difficult but essential. If you go through a rough patch, people are far more likely to stand by you if they have been kept informed as to the reasons why you're having problems.

In this brave new world where you can see the future so

All entrepreneurs reach a point where they decide to either give up or carry on.

clearly and where, on paper, anything is possible, you are bound to think you can do it all. But we all have to learn to be humble, to admit our mistakes, our shortcomings and – at times – our disappointment. Bloody-mindedness will occasionally be replaced by humility and self-doubt. All entrepreneurs reach a point where they decide to either give up or carry on. You may want to throw in the towel; you may even be encouraged to do so. It is at this point that nothing will see you through but your character or your belief in horoscopes.

You may have to tear up your business plan, go back to investors for more money, make people redundant, remortgage your home: only you can weigh up the risks of carrying on when retiring hurt is the easier option.

 ## Directory

The following is a list of recruitment agencies to help you build your team:

http://www.jobserve.co.uk
This is especially good if you're looking for IT staff

http://pricejam.com
Price Jamieson specialises in media recruitment

http://www.gecko-search.co.uk

A bespoke head-hunting firm specialising in new media.

http://www.bigbluedog.com

http://www.jobworld.co.uk

http://www.stepstone.com

http://www.recruitmedia.co.uk

http://www.monster.co.uk

http://www.wia.co.uk

http://www.totaljobs.com

Entrepreneur Profile   Paul Carr

1. Name

Paul Carr

2. Age

20

3. URL of your business

http://www.zingin.com

4. What is the purpose/nature of your business/website?

A human edited guide to the best of the internet, aimed at UK web users.

5. Date your business started

13th March 2000.

6. Is this your first new media venture?

No.

7. Briefly describe your previous business experience and state how useful this was in starting your site.

I founded an internet consultancy business (Zingin Media) in 1997 developing internet solutions for small/medium-sized businesses and quickly became frustrated by the difficulty we experienced in getting sites listed on the larger search engines. It seemed that the decent bits of the web were hidden amongst American teenagers' homepages and porn sites. The lack of a decent, human edited, guide to the internet led to the creation of Zingin.com

In terms of practical usefulness, the fact that we had a number of dedicated and talented designers and programmers 'on tap' meant that we could get the site up and running very quickly without the need for masses of seed capital. We were also able to use our contacts in the industry to spread the word about Zingin without paying through the nose for PR and consultancy services.

8. Briefly outline your educational qualifications. Please state which universities/colleges you got these qualifications from.

Currently A-Levels in Business Studies, Law and History but I'm currently studying for a Law degree at Nottingham Trent University.

9. Were you able to/did you try to raise seed financing from family and friends? If so, how much did you raise?

While my friends and family provided plenty of assistance and support in terms of beta testing and moral support, I was able to launch the site using the profits from the consultancy business and by maxing out my credit cards! Having said that, I certainly couldn't have got things started without the support of my family and my girlfriend.

10. Did you have any useful contacts when it came to raising finance? If so, what kind of introductions proved to be the most useful?

Not unless you count Barclaycard! Some of our consultancy clients put us in touch with potential investors but we, perhaps unsurprisingly, weren't able to find anyone who shared our vision for the site and who could see beyond short term profits.

11. Roughly how much money did you raise in venture capital and was this enough?

To date we have not received any VC funding. I am a very strong believer in retaining as much control of the business as possible even if it means having to live without glass-fronted offices off Oxford Street and having to compete with inferior sites with superior marketing budgets. Having said that, we are starting to look for funding to expand our full-time team and to raise our profile but I don't think VCs are necessarily the best way for us to go.

12. How many people were there on your management team?

Until recently it was just me and a team of very talented freelance designers, programmers and web surfers. The growing popularity of the site means that we have had to start building a full-time management team, most of whom have been recruited from our freelance network.

13. How useful have you found networking events like First Tuesday and Boob Night?

I don't want to have a go at networking events as though I'm sure that some people have secured funding through First Tudesday *et al.*, but they don't really hold a huge attraction for me. I went to a couple of the early First Tuesday gatherings which seemed to be like youth clubs for groovy internet folk to compare mobile phones and to show off about how much profit they weren't making. Having said that, I have found the First Tuesday email group to be very useful as many of the movers and shakers in the industry seem to lurk on it and we've been able to make some excellent contacts.

14. What would you do diferently if you had to start all over again?

It's a bit early to have regrets but if I could turn back time I would have launched the site three years ago before the web got quite so cluttered.

15. What do you think are the criteria that have most helped you make a success of your business?

Offering a large degree of human contact to our visitors. We were the first UK site to provide a team of human search guides who will help visitors track down information on the internet.

This type of one-to-one contact has allowed us to form a very strong relationship with our visitors and has led to excellent word-of-mouth advertising. I'm pretty sure Yahoo! doesn't receive as many thank you letters as we do!

16. What's been the hardest thing you've had to face since starting your business?

Personally the hardest thing for me has been trying to set up Zingin on a shoestring budget whilst juggling a law degree and trying to find time for my friends and family. Other than that, it has been very difficult to make people aware of our site in the face of competition from some very very large competitors.

17. What's the most useful piece of advice you've ever been given?

My parents advised me to retain as much ownership of Zingin as possible rather than teaming up with a partner. It's been harder work and there's no one to blame for bad decisions. Without being able to make my own decisions it would have been very difficult to get the site up and running in so little time.

18. What's the one piece of advice you wish someone had given you, but didn't?

Not to try to be all things to all people. Initially we planned to offer forums, free e-mail and a whole raft of very clichéd portal-type features. Through trial and error however (and a fair chunk of wasted time and money) we realised that people use Zingin to find the best of the web quickly and easily – they don't want to hang around all day.

19. Do you believe it's still possible for someone with only a good idea and determination to succeed in new media – or is it all about raising money these days?

It's certainly harder than it once was. The days of building a site and waiting for the money to roll in are long gone but I believe that as long as you have an original idea and enough money to get it off the ground you can still succeed without masses of VC money.

The rules of new media are starting to fall in line with those of traditional business and those e-businesses which succeed will be those who meet a real demand instead of just doing something cool on the web.

The way I see it is that if a 20-year-old law student can build a successful site on a reasonably limited budget then there's still plenty of opportunity for everyone else.

20. Are you in profit?

Nope. Like most sites which rely on advertising and sponsorship as a primary revenue source, we have still some way to go before we can all retire to our own private island.

Currently the consultancy business is subsidising Zingin.com but, with the launch of some pretty exciting business-to-business and business-to-consumer services over the next few months, we should be seeing some black ink before too long.

10 Converting paper millions into cash

IT'S NOT ONLY YOU WHO wants to turn your paper millions into cold hard cash. So do your investors. Internet economy is based on companies growing extremely fast and being floated on the stock market at the speed of light. Put a million in now and take home 10 in eight months' time seems to be the general rule. But while your investor will get to realise his investment at IPO, the chances are that you will not. While e-entrepreneurs can turn pennies into pounds far more quickly than entrepreneurs in conventional businesses, it still takes a couple of years.

Many internet millionaires are only rich on paper. The potential growth of the internet and their business can put multi-million pound price tags on their companies when they are still burning investors' cash and losing money fast. internet companies that have never made a profit – Freeserve, Lastminute.com – have floated in the UK for figures in the billion pound region largely on the back of promises. The founders' shares at flotation may be worth tens of millions, but by the time they are allowed to sell their shares they could be worth nothing.

'I think we're all in it to get out in four years' time, aren't we?' says one director of a financial services site. 'The only reason any of us could work as hard as we do is because we believe it is temporary.' So what are the routes to long summers in St Tropez and winters in Rio?

The first answer is the one you don't want to hear: more hard work. To make millions you have to do one thing: maximise. You must maximise your number of visitors, the number of visitors you convert to customers, your site's short-term profitability and long-term profitability. You must maximise not just your revenue, but the quality of your staff, your product, the number of people who have heard of you and you must maximise the envy your rivals feel towards you. Maximisation is the common denominator shared by all successful dotcom entrepreneurs.

To make millions you have to do one thing: maximise your number of visitors, the number of visitors you convert to customers, your site's short-term profitability and long-term profitability.

While it is possible to grow the potential of a start-up to massive proportions within six months of launch and get the stock market to put a £100 million price tag on your company, you won't be able to cash in your shares for some time. And this means you will have to stay with, motivate and grow your company to add real value and return real profits otherwise your share price will fall and your shares won't be worth much.

The quick route to becoming an internet millionaire is either investing via the Alternative Investment Market (AIM) and getting lucky or, like the shovel sellers in the gold rush, by selling an essential service to entrepreneurs. Hence the high valuations of incubators and some of the PR firms with internet clients. For those who run real dotcoms, however, it all takes a wee bit longer. These are the usual routes to realising your cash.

Floating your company on the stock market

An Initial Public Offering, or stock market flotation, allows the public and institutional investors such as pension fund managers to buy shares in your company. Only a proportion of your company is likely to be floated and if you have done well you can bet that your share offer will be oversubscribed, which pushes up the share price. IPOs are the best way to raise massive amounts of cash. An IPO will almost certainly dilute your shareholding, but the smaller slice of the pie you will subsequently own will be worth more. You will not be able to sell your share of the company at this point since the loss of a founder or CEO at this stage would cause the share price to crash. Typically you will be expected to hang around for the next two to five years. And to keep you motivated and devoted, investors want you to be as driven by profits as they

are and so you must keep your stake for the time being.

There are several markets you can choose to float on. The main London market, the London Stock Exchange which trades in the FTSE 100 companies, is highly regulated and sets standards and thresholds companies must meet before being allowed to trade. These include having a minimum capitalisation of £50 million and offering to trade at least £20 million of new or existing shares. You can also float on the AIM, OFEX (the unregulated off exchange market) or EASDAQ (a European market), NASDAQ (the US technology market) or

TechMARK, the technology part of the main Stock Exchange. Exchanges of any kind are regulated and complicated and you will need to appoint an accountant and broker to guide you through this process. *http://www.londonstockexchange.com* offers comprehensive information detailing the requirements of the various UK markets.

 ## Mergers

It is anticipated that 90 per cent of internet start-ups will no longer be in existence by their second birthday.

It is anticipated that 90 per cent of internet start-ups will no longer be in existence by their second birthday. This doesn't necessarily mean that they will all have folded. With all the 'me too' ideas floating around in cyberspace, often the only way to succeed is to stop competing and join forces. It is possible that, in a merger of minnows, little or no money will change hands, but if you merge with a bigger company you can expect to have a significant slice of shares as part of your salary package, as well as a cash incentive for making the deal. In other situations, a rival may want to buy your supply deals, distribution deals and customers but want you out of the picture. It's not pleasant, but your pay-off should soften the blow.

Trade sales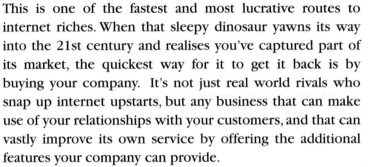

This is one of the fastest and most lucrative routes to internet riches. When that sleepy dinosaur yawns its way into the 21st century and realises you've captured part of its market, the quickest way for it to get it back is by buying your company. It's not just real world rivals who snap up internet upstarts, but any business that can make use of your relationships with your customers, and that can vastly improve its own service by offering the additional features your company can provide.

Most trade sales don't just include the purchase of stock and assets, they also include the purchase of key personnel. You can be expected to be tied into a long management agreement with your new owner that will prevent you from selling your stake in the company for many years.

Entrepreneur Profile | Robert Norton

1. Name
Robert Norton

2. Age
28

3. URL of your business
www.clickmango.com

4. What is the purpose/nature of your business/website?
Online natural health and well-being service offering a broad mix of content, commerce and community to consumers.

5. Date your business started
September 1999.

6. Is this your first new media venture?
It's my first business although I have worked for more than three years in new media, first with AOL as business development manager and head of e-commerce and then as business development director at a French search engine start-up called Nomade.

7. Briefly describe your previous business experience and state how useful this was in starting your site.

AOL was a brilliant place to learn about online business models and Nomade.fr gave me the freedom to direct the strategic growth of a business.

8. Briefly outline your educational qualifications. Please state which universities/colleges you got these qualifications from.

City of London School, 9 GCSEs, 1 AO Level, 3 A Levels.
Exeter College, Oxford, MA Oxon – Modern History.

9. Were you able to/did you try to raise seed financing from family and friends? If so, how much did you raise?

No.

10. Did you have any useful contacts when it came to raising finance? If so, what kind of introductions proved to be the most useful?

Yes, I already had several friends who had launched start-ups and they gave me great advice when we started approaching the different VCs.

11. Roughly how much money did you raise in venture capital and was this enough?

Our first round was for £3 million with Atlas Venture & Lord Rothschild.

12. How many people were there on your management team?

2 people!

13. **How useful have you found networking events like First Tuesday and BoobNight?**

First Tuesday was great at the time we were raising finance and indeed, we met the financiers from Atlas for the first time at a First Tuesday event.

14. **What would you do differently if you had to start all over again?**

There are so many things one can think about doing differently but the point is always to move on, keep up your sense of energy, work hard to achieve your goals and never stop learning.

15. **What do you think are the criteria that have most helped you make a success of your business (e.g. having first mover advantage, a brilliant marketing campaign, bloody-mindedness)?**

Understanding the consumer through focus groups, strategic marketing, investing in brand and keeping a sense of fun and enjoyment in everything we do.

16. **What's been the hardest thing you've had to face since starting your business?**

Firing people.

17. **What's the most useful piece of advice you've been given?**

Concentrate on three relationships – the consumers, the staff and the investors and the rest will look after itself.

18. What's the one piece of advice you wish someone had given you, but didn't?

Always prepare for the unexpected!

19. Do you believe it's still possible for someone with only a good idea and determination to succeed in new media? Or is it all about raising money these days?

I think the world is full of people with good ideas. It's the people with determination who make chances for themselves and the lucky ones succeed. Timing is everything and if you're the right person with the right idea at the right time and are determined to succeed – you will! Of course convincing people that you have all these three qualities is the hard thing.

20. Are you in profit?

As a company that has launched its site just two months ago, we do not expect to be in profit at this stage.

GLOSSARY

Those three unholy languages of techie, money and bullshit mean that to blend in this new world you will have to camouflage yourself in a liberal coating of three letter acronyms and learn a lexicon of nonsense.

This industry, more than any other, is full of jargon. Those three unholy languages of techie, money and bullshit mean that to blend in this new world you will have to camouflage yourself in a liberal coating of three letter acronyms and learn a lexicon of nonsense. The frightening thing is that shortly, you too will start using these words as readily as you say 'what the hell does that mean' today.

ADSL Asymetric Digital Subscriber Line or a high speed, high bandwidth telephone line.

Affiliate schemes Also known as 'associate schemes', this is the marketing strategy originally developed by Amazon to sell more books. Basically it's a commission deal whereby sites who refer customers to Amazon – and now countless other retailers – earn between five and 15 per cent of the cover price of books Amazon sells to those customers.

AIM The Alternative Investment Market, an alternative to the main Stock Exchange where companies can raise money with fewer restrictions.

Angel A business angel is someone who has made a lot of money on their own venture and now offers seed financing and advice to start-ups.

B2B Business-to-business.

B2C Business-to-consumer.

Bandwidth The capactity of fibre optic, coaxial and copper cables which carry information. The bigger the bandwidth, the faster information will transmit along a cable.

Banner The standard shape for an advertisement on a website. The standard size is 468 pixels by 60 pixels.

BIG 5 The Big 5 are the City's main accountancy firms Andersen, PriceWaterhouseCoopers, Deloitte and Touche, Ernst & Young and KPMG.

Bps Bits per second, the speed by which modems are measured.

Browser The piece of software that reads HTML. The best known versions are Netscape Navigator and internet Explorer.

Business plan The document you prepare that sets out the predicted growth of your company. Usually this document is used to raise finance from investors.

BVCA The British Venture Capital Association.

C2C Consumer-to-consumer, usually in reference to an auction site where members of the public can buy other users' property.

Carried interest A 'carried interest scheme' allows employees of venture capital companies to co-invest in companies, usually on favourable terms.

Cash rich A company that says it is 'cash rich' basically means it has a positive cash flow, i.e. its income exceeds its expenditure.

Click-through The rate at which users click on banner ads to visit another, usually an advertiser's, site is known as the click-through rate and is typically less than 1 per cent. i.e. for every 100 visitors only one person clicks on the banner.

Comfort factor Investors try and make themselves as 'comfortable' as possible when investing by investigating your company as fully as possible to reach the comfort factor.

Completion The point at which legal documents between your company and an investor are signed, usually the point at which money is transferred into your account.

CPM Cost per thousand. The common rate for calculating advertising costs.

CRM Customer relationship management. Something the web is supposed to be good at.

Deal flow   The rate at which business plans flow through the offices of venture capital firms.

Deferred consideration   This is when elements of deals only come into play if certain targets are met, e.g. an investor will give you money when your income reaches an agreed level.

Dilution   This is what happens to your share of your company when you issue shares to someone else. Instead of owning 100 per cent, your share is diluted to, say, 50 per cent or 10 per cent. Some investors put in non-dilution clauses into contracts which means that their share isn't diluted by future rounds of investment.

Domain   The officially registered URL of your site, e.g. *http://www.howtonetamillion.com.*

Draw down   This is when an investor commits him/herself to a certain amount of funds, but you are only able to 'draw down' a limited amount in any given time period.

Due diligence   This is the detailed analysis of claims, predictions and assumptions in a business plan carried out before investment is made, usually after a deal has been agreed in principle. References are taken on the management team and the legal and financial standing of the company is investigated.

E-commerce   Electronic commerce, i.e. selling stuff over the net.

Equity   Ownership of a company is held in equity stakes.

EVCA   The European Venture Capital Association.

Exit   The opportunity your investor will take to recoup his investment in your company. Typically an IPO or a trade sale.

Flash   Usually a flashy site has been developed using a piece of software called Flash which allows complicated animations. Some sites are now being built entirely using Flash.

Flip   A short-term investment whereby an investor plans a quick Exit. Sometimes that Exit can be agreed prior to Completion.

FTP   File Transfer Protocol, the most common method of uploading content from your computer to your Server.

GIF   One of the most common formats for web images.

Hamster wheel   A situation many entrepreneurs find themselves in when they can't reach critical mass without investment and can't get investment until they reach critical mass.

Hands on   When an investor gets involved in the running of your company. Hands off, funnily enough, is when an investor lets you get on with your job without interference.

Hit Possibly the single most misused word in the web dictionary. Hits are often used to describe the level of Traffic experienced by a website but they are misleading as a site that has 250,000 hits per week may only have a few thousand visitors. A 'hit' is registered every time a user downloads an image or block of text from a site. Just looking at one page can register 20 or more hits. A more accurate Traffic measurement is the Page Impression.

Hockey stick The ideal shape of your company's growth chart: an initial dip as investment is spent followed by a long upward stroke as profits rise.

Horizontal A horizontal company has a flat structure that often provides the same service or function at the same level across geographies or industries.

Host A company that holds your site on their Server.

Hyperlink A piece of text on a website that is underlined and links to another page.

HTML Stands for Hyper Text Mark-up Language, a code that allows links to be placed from one page on the web to another.

Incorporation The term used for becoming a limited company.

Incubator A company that offers Seed financing and strategic advice to Start-ups.

Intellectual property This is often property which it is difficult to put a monetary value on, and includes assets like patents, brand names etc.

IPO Initial Public Offering, or flotation on the stock markets.

ISDN High speed phone line.

ISP Internet Service Provider, e.g. Freeserve, AOL or Demon.

JPEG One of the most common formats for web images.

JV A joint venture.

Lead investor When several investors come onboard as a syndicate, one investor will act as the negotiator for all the other investors. He/she is the lead investor.

Listing A placing on the Stock Exchange.

M-commerce Mobile commerce. i.e. allowing people to buy stuff on the move through their mobile phones.

Message board A place on a website where you can leave a message that other people can respond to.

NDA No disclosure agreement, or confidentiality notice.

Newbie An annoying word for people who are new to the net.

Newsgroup   Traditionally, an academic and sophisticated message board.

Noise   The confused sound made by lots of websites all screaming for attention.

Options   Stock options are incentives given (usually) to staff that allow them to buy a specified number of shares after a specified date at a specified price (usually the price shares were when they joined the company). Typically options are vested in stages which means the longer an employee stays with a company the more Options he/she is allowed to own.

Page impression   The most common Traffic measurement advertisers are interested in. A page impression records how many times users have requested a certain page.

Portal   One of the web's most overused terms, a portal is a site that provides a window into the web. Typically these are Search Engines and Directories, but increasingly there are industry-specific portals which are a one-stop shop for people working in a specific industry.

Preferential shares   When second round investors put in millions of pounds for relatively (in comparison to first round investors) small equity stakes, they are usually compensated with preferential shares which give them, for instance, the same voting rights as a much larger stakeholder.

Radar screen   The phrase is usually 'below our radar screen' and means that something is too small to be of interest.

Search engine   A website that helps you find other websites by keying in certain words which it then searches for. It's estimated that only 7 per cent of websites are listed or spidered by search engines.

Seed financing   Sometimes called the first round of finance, this is often a few hundred thousand pounds raised from family and friends, business angels and Incubators.

Sensitivities   The things that – if they change – can most affect your business.

Server   A computer that holds your website on it and can be accessed 24 hours a day.

Share placing   The sale of shares to specified investors but not the general public.

Space   When people talk about 'occupying space' they mean claiming a share of the market for their company.

Spam   Junk email.

Start-up   A new company.

Syndicate   A group of investors who take equity in a company at the same time and get the same deal. It is not necessary for the syndicate to meet or know each other.

Synergy If you have synergy with another company, this means your businesses could work well together.

Trade sale The purchase of your company by another company.

Traffic The term for people who visit your site.

Unique visitor This Traffic measurement records the number of times any single domain name, or IP address, visited your site in a 24 hour period. Depending on your stats program, this may count each person from the same IP address, or company, as one person.

Upload Sending information to your site, rather than getting it (downloading it) from someone else's site.

URL A Universal Resource Locator, otherwise known as your domain name.

Valuation Just about the hardest term to define in the internet world as valuations in companies that aren't publicly floated are spurious. Valuation is an art, not a science.

Vertical A vertical company is one that owns a product or a concept from inception to delivery.

Vortal A vertical portal.

Vulture capitalist A greedy or ruthless venture capitalist.

WAP Wireless Application Protocol; the mobile equivalent of HTML.

INDEX